TURNING POINTS
In the World's History.

BY
HENRY MANN.

AUTHOR OF
"The Land We Live In," etc

Fredonia Books
Amsterdam, The Netherlands

Turning Points In the World's History

by
Henry Mann

ISBN: 1-58963-646-5

Copyright © 2002 by Fredonia Books

Reprinted from the 1897 edition,
Originally Published by the Christian Herald

Fredonia Books
Amsterdam, The Netherlands
http://www.fredoniabooks.com

All rights reserved, including the right to reproduce this book, or portions thereof, in any form.

In order to make original editions of historical works available to scholars at an economical price, this facsimile of the original edition of 1897 is reproduced from the best available copy and has been digitally enhanced to improve legibility, but the text remains unaltered to retain historical authenticity.

INTRODUCTORY.

The path of human progress has witnessed many turning-points from the time when superior intellect taught man that he was different from the brute. In religion, in literature, in science the forward march has been one of difficulty, of pain, of sacrifice. Religion is not alone in the precious heritage of martyrs who have endured and perished for the truth. Every line of invention, of learning, of thought beyond the present, and of aspiration for the improvement of mankind, has had its martyrs, and in the end its victors. The turning-points in history are a record of human suffering, of human effort, and of human triumph and achievement, under the control of that providence which guides the affairs of men.

* * * * * * * * *

I have sought to indicate in these pages some of the leading occurrences that have influenced the destinies of humanity, confining myself chiefly to events connected with and subsequent to the dawn of enlightenment in the fifteenth century. I have sought to trace the causes and course of the Reformation, of the French Revolution, and of the other great turning-points in

Introductory.

the beginnings of great inventions, and their influence upon modern conditions have not been neglected.

* * * * * * *

As war is the ultimate court of appeal in human affairs, it follows that the battlefield has often been a turning-point in history. Engagements by land and sea have decided the fate of nations, loosed the bonds of tyranny or riveted the chain of despotism. A single battle has sometimes halted manifest destiny, as Joshua halted the sun in its inevitable course, for centuries. The battle of Bannockburn was an instance of this. That England and Scotland should some day become united was as certain in the days of Edward the Second as any event not accomplished. The resolute valor of Bruce and the courage of his followers postponed that union for three centuries, and then it was brought about as a peaceful consequence of the accident of royal succession.

It does not follow that what is known as a decisive battle has been the turning-point of the historic episode of which that battle was the conclusion, but it is only natural that the human mind should commonly associate great changes with prominent events. But for Moscow Napoleon would, in all human probability, have never had to confront the British at Waterloo. Nevertheless Waterloo decided his fate, and relieved Europe from the scourge of his ambition. In this sense, and for this reason, Waterloo will always be regarded as the greatest military event of the century, in the Old World at least.

The defeat and destruction of the "Invincible Armada" merits a place in these pages because it secured to England superiority to Spain on the seas, and prevented a Roman Catholic conquest of the leading Protestant kingdom. The story of Pultowa can be read intelligently only in the light of Lutzen. Pultowa brought the Swedish empire to an end, and established the power of Russia on an enduring foundation.

Since Waterloo the world has witnessed in Europe two decisive battles—Koniggratz and Sedan, the first of which established, and the second confirmed, the unity of Germany.

Turning to our own land the struggle for the possession of Fort Duquesne, ending in the retreat of the French, decided that the British race should dominate North America. Burgoyne's surrender at Saratoga was the turning-point against England in the War of Independence. The battle of Lake Erie secured the Northwest to the United States, and put an end to the dream of an Indian power nursed by Great Britain, a mosquito monarchy on the shores of Lake Superior. There yet remained to be decided whether Anglo-Americans or Spanish-Americans should be the Romans of the western hemisphere. The Mexican war, with its decisive battle of Cerro Gordo, settled that question so thoroughly that it has never since been raised, and is never likely to be raised again.

Then came our great civil war, with Gettysburg as its decisive battle. The American people, both North and South, have reason to be proud of the valor displayed on that fateful day. May the future turning-points of our nation be only in the direction of peace—save when peace would involve dishonor.

HENRY MANN.

August, 1897.

CONTENTS.

	PAGE.
I.—THE BIRTH OF THE SAVIOUR,	9
II.—CANOSSA AND THE RIALTO,	16

    The Triple Crown—An Imperial Suppliant—The Rialto—The Pope's Heel on Cæsar's Neck—Papal Absolutism.

III.—THE FIRST BIBLE PRINTED,	28
IV.—GUNPOWDER VERSUS CHIVALRY,	33
V.—VASCO DAGAMA'S VOYAGE,	37
VI.—FIRST VOYAGE OF COLUMBUS,	43
VII.—SPAIN'S EXPULSION OF THE JEWS,	59
VIII.—THE REFORMATION,	66

    Erasmus—Luther—Charles V.—The Reformation in Germany — The Reformation in England — The Reformation in Scotland — The Reformation in Holland — The Reformation in Sweden—The Reformation in France.

IX.—TRIAL OF THE SEVEN BISHOPS,	84
X.—HUTCHINSON'S WRITS OF ASSISTANCE,	93
XI.—THE GUILLOTINE VERSUS THE DIVINE RIGHT OF KINGS,	110

    Why Napoleon Failed.

XII.—THE MONROE DECLARATION,	127

Contents.

                                                         PAGE.

XIII.—England's Commercial Turning-Point, ... 134
    Peel Launches Free Trade.

XIV.—Lincoln's Death-Blow to Slavery, ... 140

XV.—The Geneva Tribunal, ... 148
    Arbitration's First Victory.

XVI.—Industrial Turning-Points, . . . 162
    Watt Makes Steam Work—Murdock Gives Light—Fulton Ploughs the Hudson—Stephenson's "Rocket" Flies—Franklin Draws the Lightning—Morse's Happy Thought—Cyrus Field's First Cable Message—Bell and Edison Make Lightning Talk—Electric Light and Power—Cotton Spinning Machinery—Arkwright in England—Slater in America.

XVII.—Ten Military and Naval Turning-Points, ... 193
    Europe.—Destruction of the Spanish Armada—Pultowa—Waterloo—Koniggratz—Sedan. *America.*—Duquesne—Saratoga—Lake Erie—Cerro Gordo—Gettysburg.

XVIII.—Great Religious Movements of the Century, ... 281

TURNING POINTS
IN THE
WORLD'S HISTORY.

I.—THE BIRTH OF THE SAVIOUR.

The birth of Christ was the greatest turning-point of history. It was the first chapter in the gospel of a new dispensation—the gospel of common rights, common duties, a common manhood and common fraternity. The Christianity of the earlier days was typified in the stable at Bethlehem. According to the belief of Christians, the Saviour of mankind might have been born in a palace on the Tiber, or in the proudest residence of Herod the Great, but He elected to come as one of the vast, unnumbered multitude of unknown toilers who, for ages before and since His coming, have been trodden under foot of the rich, the noble and the powerful. In this He asserted at once the supremacy of God and the dignity and the equality of man. The birth of Christ was the first and eloquent declaration of our human brotherhood. It was a protest from Divinity itself against the artificial barriers of caste and class, erected, like the Tower of Babel, to overcome the decrees of heaven.

It has been said, as an objection to Christianity, that Christ is not mentioned outside of sacred history. No higher tribute could be paid to the Saviour and Messiah. He did not belong—He did not choose to belong—to the class of whom history, or at least ancient history, recorded the deeds and achievements. He did not wade through a Rubicon of blood to a dictatorship, or sweep with embattled armies over desolated provinces, amid the anguish of women and children and the ruins of uncounted homes. Ah no! Christ did not make history of that kind. His part was cast with the myriads who from the beginning of the world had been the victims of the history-makers, whose sufferings and sacrifices are known only to the Omniscient, and whose names have passed into oblivion with their unmonumented graves. Christ came as one of these. He was of them and with them. From among them He chose His disciples, and among them He gained His followers, and through their faithful ranks He made His triumphal way on that final ride to Jerusalem, the Passion and the Cross. The name and the career of Christ would have been out of place in the chronicles of the Cæsars and the pages which tell the story of Roman conquest and oppression.

* * * * * * *

CHRIST'S MISSION TO THE LOWLY.

It was undoubtedly this mighty lesson of man's equality as taught by Christ in the very moment of His birth that excited the intense and fierce opposition of the powerful and privileged classes in Judea, and subsequently in Rome, against the Christians. The antagonism to early Christianity was based, not on religious differences, but on social and political grounds. Every instinct of wealth, power and authority became arrayed against a creed which taught that the poor man was as good as the rich man, the serf the equal of the emperor; that it was the duty of those who had, to share with those who had not. First to the Pharisee, as afterward to the Roman Cæsar and his parasites, Christian doctrine appeared subversive of the very foundations of society. The Christians were persecuted, not because they did not believe in the gods of Olympus, but because they held Cæsar to be no better, as a man, than anybody else, and because they held it to be the duty of Dives to divide with Lazarus, and for all to labor for the common welfare. The idea of worshiping as God one who had been born in a stable and laid in a manger, who had worked as a carpenter and then turned preacher, and who had told the rich and fortunate to sell their goods and give to the poor, impressed the Luculluses, the nobles, the kings, emperors and priests of that age, as a menace to the very foundations of the state, and a defiance of the classes who made ordinary mankind the slaves of their appetites and the ministers of their caprice.

At the same time the very doctrine of human equality and the brotherhood of man, which raised all the dominant forces of ancient society against the stable-born Christ, made Christianity invincible. The millions had been waiting and hungering for just such a Deliverer. The Jews never expected their Messiah to come in that guise, but the common people, both Jew and Gentile, were quick to understand the Saviour because He understood them, and the same touch of heart to heart which drew multitudes to Jesus in His lifetime drew multitudes to His apostles when they went among the nations with their mission from the manger and the cross. Christianity was the people's faith. It did not spread down to the people from the classes above them, but gradually won recruits from the higher ranks by the example of self-denial, charity and purity, illustrated in the Christian community.

Persecution, intolerance and every form of temptation, could not quench the star that rose over the sleeping Babe in that lonely stable in Bethlehem. The sword of Herod sought in vain to destroy the newborn Christ, although hundreds of innocents perished that the fears of the tyrant might be allayed. What a cruel sacrifice! What awful evidence of the depth of degradation and oppression to which even the chosen people had sunk under the ruthless despotism of the wretches who wore the crown of David and of Solomon! What a picture of the condition of the class among whom Christ chose to be born, and to whom His birth was the morning light of deliverance! Helpless in the grasp of their oppressors, their children put to the sword to gratify the whim of a monster, and burdened almost beyond endurance by the exactions of usurer and tax-gatherer, the common people of that age had no rights that were regarded as paramount to the absolute will of the despots who scourged them. Judaism had become loaded down with forms and ceremonies, and its religion was a gilded skeleton of the once vigorous faith which had animated the Israelites in heroic struggle against their hereditary foes. The Romans held them in bondage and looked upon them with contempt, while permitting the degenerate rulers who exercised the worst form of Eastern tyranny over their miserable subjects to retain the thrones which they stained by the most inhuman excesses. Judea had lost its independence without gaining as an equivalent the firm and impartial government which the Romans usually bestowed on subject provinces. The age was ripe for a Saviour, and nowhere riper than in Judea.

* * * * * * * * *

Looked at from its human consequences alone, the birth of the Saviour was the most momentous event in the annals of mankind. The Christianity born in that stable did not change human nature, but even alloyed as it afterward became, it gave a higher, purer, more inspiring and more exalting religious ideal than the world had ever known. However absurd the divisions among Christians of the earlier centuries on technical points of doctrine may appear to us now, the Christian ideal was at least always and entirely free from the impurity and depravity which characterized the imaginary population of Olympus. The Christians offered a God who could be worshiped without blush or reservation, a Christ who appealed to the noblest sentiments and to the purest sympathies, a faith which rested on divine love as its cornerstone and brotherly love and charity as the chief pillars of its creed.

Men learned that there was something to hope for, something to gain, which Cæsar and his legions could not achieve, which a tyrant's tortures could not tear from them, which the fires of persecution could not reduce to ashes. They learned that the world, its ambitions, its strife and its fleeting indulgences, were as vapor compared with the promise of everlasting bliss in the bosom of the ever-loving God; that the pomp and parade of royalty and riches were to the wealth of the purified soul as tinsel to the stars, and that the poorest slave in Iberian mines might, if he lived a Christ-like life, stand nearer the throne of God than the ruler of an empire.

No wonder that doctrine such as this amazed and aroused the masters of ancient civilization, and that from the banks of the Tiber to the frontiers of Parthia the fires were lighted and the irons were heated to efface from the earth a religion which taught that Cæsar was brother to his serfs. And the struggle went on from emperor to emperor, from century to century, between all the powers of the known world on the one side and the zeal of undying faith, the supreme confidence of imperishable love, on the other side—and at length the Nazarene was conqueror, the manger triumphed, the Babe of Bethlehem became the Romans' God.

II.—CANOSSA AND RIALTO.

It is a long step from Bethlehem to Canossa; it is a long step from Constantine to Canossa, and from the bishop of Rome, who called himself "servant of the servants of God," to the Pope with his heel on the neck of an emperor. I have no room in this book to trace the origin of the papal power. The supremacy of the Roman See appears to have been generally recognized by the Western churches for centuries before the great Hildebrand came upon the scene, and sought to convert that supremacy into an absolutism, both spiritual and temporal. In the view of the vast majority of believers, the spiritual weapon hurled by the hand of the successor of St. Peter was as vivid as the lightning's flash, and much more terrible, for the lightning could only kill the body, while the papal anathema doomed both soul and body to everlasting torments. Occasionally a prince, intoxicated by the adulation of parasites, and the possession of unlimited power over the property and lives of millions of subjects, challenged the hostility of the pope, and he might, perhaps, achieve a momentary success, but every day his cause was sure to become weaker and less hopeful. Natural calamities were regarded as expressions of divine displeasure, and the very stars in their courses seemed to be warring against him. His trusted confidants, who might have recklessly applauded his resolution and courage in the beginning, shrank from his presence as from that of a leper, and the loyalty of his subjects was chilled by the thought that their prince was the enemy of God. His mind was irritated, his conscience tortured, and at length life appeared to be intolerable without reconciliation to the Vicar of Christ.

Such was the condition of Christendom when Hildebrand, a monk, the son of a carpenter of Siena, in Tuscany, obtained an ascendency in the papal court. Hildebrand was one of those men who, in the ever-moving caravan of historical characters, loom above their contemporaries like a giant among pigmies. His was not a lovable nature. He possessed an unconquerable will and an inflexible singleness of purpose, combined with that magnetic force which compels the common to recognize the master mind. There is no reason to doubt his sincerity, or even to suppose that he was consciously actuated by ambitious or selfish motives. The last words of his life—"I have loved justice and hated iniquity, and therefore I die in exile"—were doubtless from his heart. To him the cause of the Church was the cause of justice; its defeat

the triumph of iniquity. Hildebrand aimed
to carry out to its logical conclusion the
doctrine that the pope is the Vicar of Christ
upon earth; that the papal authority being
of divine origin is superior to any earthly
jurisdiction, and that the Roman pontiff, in
virtue of his sacred office, is invested with
the power to direct and govern all affairs,
both spiritual and temporal. He essayed
to establish through his legates papal super-
vision over the strictly secular acts of sovereign princes, to summon them to his feet
to answer accusations of maladministration,
and, in a word, to make Christendom one
vast theocracy, with the pope as the inter-
preter and oracle of the divine will. He
endeavored to sever all ties which bound
the ecclesiastical order to the service of the
State, and to make the State the servant,
as he claimed it to be, the creature of the
Church. He tried to enforce the most rigid
celibacy, so that the priesthood might not
be diverted by the vexations and pleasures
of the family relation from the single object
of the aggrandizement of the pontificate.

In 1073, the son of the carpenter of Siena
ascended the chair of St. Peter, and assumed the title of Gregory VII. He spent
the early period of his pontificate in enforc-
ing stricter discipline among the clergy,
and in strengthening himself for the coming struggle with the young and arrogant

emperor of Germany. Henry IV. was a brave and successful soldier, but he was of resentful disposition, hasty and unstable in action, and licentious in conduct. His extravagances kept him always in want of money, and he replenished his treasury by the sale of episcopal sees to incapable and unworthy men. Gregory admonished the emperor to cease his simoniacal practices but without effect. In 1074 the pope summoned a council at Rome, which pronounced an anathema against all persons guilty of simony, and likewise ordered the deposition of priests who lived in concubinage. In 1075 another council prohibited princes, under pain of excommunication, from giving investiture of sees or abbeys, by conferring the ring and crosier.

The emperor continued to dispose of the episcopal dignity and emoluments for money, without heeding the admonition of the pontiff, or the anathema of the council. Gregory, who was now thoroughly aroused, summoned Henry to Rome, not only to account for his defiance of ecclesiastical laws, but also to answer charges of secular misgovernment preferred against him by his subjects. Henry, hotly indignant at what he considered to be a gross insult to the majesty, and encroachment upon the prerogatives of the imperial crown, caused a diet of the empire to be assembled at

Worms, which fulminated a sentence of
deposition and excommunication against
Gregory; and the emperor addressed a missive, informing the Roman pontiff of the
action of the diet, to "the false monk, Hildebrand." Gregory replied by an edict
excommunicating the emperor, depriving
him of his kingdoms of Germany and Italy,
and releasing his subjects from their allegiance, and forbidding them to obey their
sovereign. Henry soon found that he had
bearded a foe more formidable than any he
had faced on the field of battle. Disloyal
nobles rose in rebellion against him, and
claimed that they were carrying out the
will of Heaven in attacking a monarch accursed by the Vicar of Christ. Henry was
deserted by the prelates who had aided in
his attempt to drive Gregory from the papal
throne, but who now hastened to make
peace with their ecclesiastical Cæsar. Even
the near friends of the emperor avoided
his presence, and he found himself a prince
without courtiers, a ruler without subjects.
He sank from the height of arrogance into
utter despondency, and resolved, as a last
desperate resort, to throw himself on the
mercy of the Roman pontiff.

AN IMPERIAL SUPPLIANT.

Accompanied by his faithful Bertha and
a single attendant, Henry crossed the Alps,

and proceeded to Canossa, a fortress near Reggio, where Gregory was the guest of his devoted adherent, the Countess Matilda. The emperor was admitted into an outer court of the castle, and remained there from morning until evening, for three successive days, clad in a shirt of hair, and with naked feet, while Gregory, shut up with the countess, appeared to ignore his presence. On the fourth day the pope condescended to grant absolution to his humbled enemy, but on condition that he should not resume the insignia of imperial power until the pontiff had determined whether or not his kingdoms should be restored to him.

* * * * * * * * *

Canossa did not bring an end to the struggle between pope and emperor, which was soon resumed, and continued with varying fortunes. The conflict reached its fiercest point when Frederick Barbarossa directed all the power of the German empire to the crushing of Pope Alexander III. The pope wandered from court to court, from kingdom to kingdom, a fugitive and a suppliant, vainly begging the princes of Christendom to champion the cause of the Church, while the fairest regions of Italy were desolated by contending armies shouting the war cry of "Guelph!" or "Ghibelin!"

The decisive battle of Legnano, when the
imperial army was totally crushed by the
forces of the Guelphic confederacy, did not
break the proud spirit of Frederick. When
the Venetians, in behalf of Alexander,
made overtures to Barbarossa with a view
to an amicable settlement, he answered:
"Go and tell your prince and his people
that Frederick, king of Romans, demands
at their hands a fugitive and a foe; that,
if they refuse to deliver him to me, I shall
deem and declare them the enemies of my
empire; and that I will pursue them by
land and by sea, until I have planted my
victorious eagles on the gates of St.
Mark's."

The islanders were not daunted by this
arrogant menace, and they got ready to
make a desperate defence against the
armada which, under Otho Hohenstauffen,
the son of the emperor, was preparing to
invade their lagoons. The Venetians met
the squadron of Barbarossa off Salboro,
seven miles distant from Pirano (May 26,
1177). The imperialists numbered seventy-
five sail; the islanders only thirty-four;
but the latter were inspired by every motive that could nerve the arm or stimulate
the courage. The fight lasted for six
hours, and ended in the utter rout of the
imperial fleet. Otho himself was captured,
and forty of his vessels fell into the hands

of the conquerors, besides two which foundered during the action. Pope Alexander met the victors at the landing-place on their return, and in token of his appreciation of their invaluable services to his cause, he bestowed upon Venice the perpetual dominion of the ocean.

POPE'S HEEL ON CÆSAR'S NECK.

Barbarossa was now willing to listen to the proposals which he had so wrathfully rejected but a few months before, and it was arranged that a congress should meet at Rialto and discuss and ratify the terms of peace. The emperor likewise signified his desire to be readmitted within the pale of the Church, and Alexander acceded to his request. Frederick arrived in Venice on the twenty-third of July, and was received in a manner befitting his imperial station, and the dignity of the republic of which he was the guest. On the morning of the twenty-fourth, a procession of the doge, nobles and clergy of Venice escorted Barbarossa to St. Mark's, where the pope sat in state, arrayed in his pontifical robes, and surrounded by the ambassadors of Sicily, France and England, the delegates of the free cities and a throng of peers and cardinals, bishops and archbishops. Assuming a lowly attitude the emperor approached the papal throne, and, casting off his purple mantle, prostrated himself before the pope. The sufferings and persecutions of eighteen years recurred at that moment to the memory of His Holiness, and a sincere and profound conviction that he was the instrument chosen of Heaven to proclaim the predestined triumph of right might have actuated the pontiff, as he planted his foot on the neck of the emperor, and borrowing the words of David, cried: "Thou shalt go on the lion and the adder; the young lion and the dragon shalt thou tread under thy feet." "It is not to thee, but to St. Peter, that I kneel," muttered the fallen tyrant. "Both to me and to St. Peter," insisted Ranuci, pressing his heel still more firmly on the neck of Frederick; and as soon as the latter appeared to acquiesce, the pope relaxed his hold, and suffered His Majesty to rise.

A Te Deum closed this remarkable ceremony, and, on quitting the cathedral, the emperor held the sacred stirrup, and assisted his tormentor to mount. Barbarossa continued ever after to be on friendly terms with Rome, and the old emperor perished in the river Calycadnus, in Cilicia, while leading the Third Crusade against the Moslems.

* * * * * * * * * *

PAPAL ABSOLUTISM.

The papal power may be said to have reached its apogee during the reign of

Innocent III., who was crowned with the tiara, after the demise of Celestine, in 1197. Born of a noble Roman family, versed in all the learning of the mediæval schools, deeply imbued with the principles to which Hildebrand had been a martyr, and yet in the flush and vigor of early manhood, the new pope speedily showed a purpose to subject the whole world to his domineering will, and to make himself the ruler of the earth, the prince of princes. In a communication to the league of Tuscan communes, Innocent averred that "as God created two luminaries, one superior for the day, and the other inferior for the night, which last owes its splendor entirely to the first, so he has disposed that the regal dignity should be but a reflection of the splendor of the papal authority, and entirely subordinate to it." He required an oath of allegiance from the prefect of Rome, thus abolishing forever the authority of the German empire over that city; he drove from the dominions of the Church the imperial feudatories and took possession of their territories in the name of the Roman See. He asserted the papal suzerainty over Sicily, and obtained from Constance, regent of that kingdom for her infant son, Frederick II., an acknowledgment of the pontifical claims; and, after the death of Constance, he himself assumed the regency.

Innocent decided the contest for the imperial throne in favor of Otho, the Guelph candidate. He afterward, in 1210, deposed Otho, and caused his own ward, young Frederick II., to be crowned emperor at Aix-la-Chapelle, with the approval of the Fourth Lateran Council. He excommunicated Philip Augustus, of France, because that monarch had repudiated his wife, Ingerburga, of Denmark, and married Agnes de Meranie. The French king persisting in his defiance of the ecclesiastical and moral law, Innocent laid an interdict upon his dominions. The performance of public worship was strictly prohibited, the churches were closed, the dying were denied the consolations of religion, and the dead lay unburied. Neither Philip nor his subjects could long sustain the horrors of such a situation, and the king relieved himself and his kingdom from the papal curse by receiving back the wife he had discarded. When Alfonso IX., of Leon and Castile, took as his queen his own niece, the daughter of Sancho, king of Portugal, Innocent first remonstrated, and when remonstrance was found to be in vain, he laid the dominions of the offending princes under interdict, and did not remove the ban until the scandal ceased.

John Lackland took an oath of fealty to the Roman See, and delivered to the papal envoy a charter testifying that he surrendered to Innocent and to his successors forever the kingdom of England and the lordship of Ireland, to be held as fiefs, on condition of the payment to the pope of a tribute of seven hundred marks of silver for England, and three hundred for Ireland. Peter II., of Aragon, voluntarily made himself a vassal of Rome, in order to secure his dynasty against the jealous ambition of his powerful lieges, and bound himself and his successors to an annual payment of two hundred pieces of gold. John, duke of Bavaria, Premislas, of Bohemia, and Leo, of Armenia, accepted kingly crowns from Innocent. John, of Bulgaria, had long boasted that he was a vassal only of the pope. Hungary was acknowledged by its monarch to be a fief of the Holy See, and Denmark bowed to the power which had vindicated the honor and avenged the wrongs of her royal daughter. Even Norway felt the weight of papal censure, and distant Iceland listened with respect and fear to the admonitions of a legate from the court of Rome.

III.—THE FIRST BIBLE PRINTED.

An agency most potent in preparing Europe for the Reformation was the invention of printing. The monkish scribes would certainly have taken no pains to spread doctrine which they considered heretical, and the people would have remained in ignorance of all arguments tending to disparage the supremacy and infallibility of Rome.

It is needless to go into the controversy as to whether Johannes Gutenberg or Laurens Coster was the pioneer of the printing-press. "While the learned of Italy," says Hallam, "were eagerly exploring their recent acquisitions of manuscripts, deciphered with difficulty, and slowly circulated from hand to hand, a few obscure Germans had gradually perfected the most important discovery recorded in the annals of mankind. The invention of printing, so far from being the result of philosophical sagacity, does not appear to have been suggested by any regard for the higher branches of literature, or to bear any other relation than that of coincidence to their revival in Italy. The question why it was struck out at that particular time must be referred to that disposition of unknown causes which we call accident.

"Two or three centuries earlier, we cannot but acknowledge, the discovery would have been almost equally acceptable. But the invention of paper seems to have naturally preceded those of engraving and printing. It is generally agreed that playing-cards, which have been traced far back in the fourteenth century, gave the first notion of taking off impressions from engraved figures upon wood. The second stage, or rather the second application, of this art, was the representation of saints and other religious devices, several instances of which are still extant. Some of these are accompanied with an entire page of illustrative text, cut into the same wooden block. This process is indeed far removed from the invention that has given immortality to the names of Faust, Schoeffer and Gutenberg, yet it probably led to the consideration of means whereby it might be rendered less operose and inconvenient.

"Whether movable wooden characters were ever employed in any entire work is very questionable—the opinion that referred their use to Laurens Coster, of Haarlem, not having stood the test of more accurate investigation. They appear, however, in the capital letters of some early printed books. But no expedient of this kind could have fulfilled the great purposes of this invention until it was perfected by pounding metal types in a matrix or mould, the essential characteristic of printing, as distinguished from other arts that bear some analogy to it.

"The first book that issued from the presses of Faust and his associates at Mentz was an edition of the Vulgate, commonly called the Mazarine Bible, a copy having been discovered in the library that owes its name to Cardinal Mazarin at Paris. This is supposed to have been printed between the years 1450 and 1455. In 1457 an edition of the Psalter appeared, and in this the invention was announced to the world in a boasting colophon, though certainly not unreasonably bold. Another edition of the Psalter, one of an ecclesiastical book, Durand's account of liturgical offices, one of the Constitutions of Pope Clement V., and one of a popular treatise on general science, called the Catholicon, filled up the interval till 1462, when the second Mentz Bible proceeded from the same printers. This, in the opinion of some, is the earliest book in which cast types were employed—those of the Mazarine Bible having been cut with the hand. But this is a controverted point.

"In 1465, Faust and Schoeffer published an edition of Cicero's Offices, the first tribute of the new art to polite literature. Two pupils of their school, Sweynheim and Pannartz, migrated the same year into Italy, and printed Donatus's grammar and the works of Lactantius at the monastery of Subiaco, in the neighborhood of Rome. Venice had the honor of extending her patronage to John, of Spira, the first who applied the art on an extensive scale to the publication of classical writers. Several authors came forth from his press in 1470; and during the next ten years a multitude of editions were published in various parts of Italy.

"Though, as we may judge from their present scarcity, these editions were by no means numerous in respect of impressions, yet, contrasted with the dilatory process of copying manuscripts, they were like a new mechanical power in machinery, and gave a wonderfully accelerated impulse to the intellectual cultivation of mankind. From the era of these first editions, proceeding from the Spiras, Zarot, Janson, or Sweynheim and Pannartz, literature must be deemed to have altogether revived in Italy. The sun was now fully above the horizon, though countries less fortunately circumstanced did not immediately catch his beams; and the restoration of ancient learning in France and England cannot be considered as by any means effectual, even at the close of the fifteenth century."

* * * * * * *

Of the tremendous influence of the printing-press in spreading religious as well as secular knowledge, we have all-sufficient evidence in the decree of the French Diocletian, Francis I., who in 1535 ordered the abolition of printing "that means of propagating heresies," and forbade the printing of any book under penalty of death. It is true that this decree, made all the more atrocious by the fact that the king who issued it was himself a man of letters, was revoked for very shame about six weeks later, but the spirit which prompted it shows that, before the printing-press had been in operation for a century, it was hated and dreaded by bigots and tyrants alike.

IV.—GUNPOWDER VS. CHIVALRY.

Hardly less important than the invention of printing was the introduction of gunpowder as an efficient agent in war. Gunpowder, or something very like it, had been known for many centuries in the East, and is even said by a Greek historian to have been used by Indian armies in the time of Alexander. The Greek-fire used to defend Constantinople against the Saracens was in composition very like gunpowder, but it was not a propellant. It was an inflammable substance, which, projected by means of arrows, or through a tube, spread destruction and confusion among the enemy. Greek-fire, however, was of little or no value in open warfare, and until gunpowder made it possible to kill at a considerable distance, the knight in armor was master of the field. Battles were fought by hand-to-hand conflict, or by archery, which decided Cressy, Agincourt and other important engagements. It is an interesting fact that the English were always superior to the French as archers, and that the French kings had to hire Scottish archers to make headway against the English. The English archers were organized in large divisions, and the dense masses of arrows falling among the foe often caused a panic, and opened the way for an effective onslaught.

It may be needless to say that the use of artillery in mediæval battles did very little damage. The victory of Cressy was due to the archers, and not to two or three smoothbore "cannon," with crude gunpowder which propelled a few balls into the hostile ranks.

While the cannon of Cressy made but little noise, they sounded the doom of chivalry. In the fifteenth century artillery came into general use, both in land and naval operations, and armor no longer presented an impregnable defence to ordinary weapons of war. Indeed, the cumbersome mail, interfering with rapid movement, and useless against artillery, became an impediment that was gradually discarded, piece by piece, save for a stout helmet and the cuirass. Suits of armor were laid aside in ancestral halls among relics of the past, and knight and peasant went forth to battle on an equal footing. Gunpowder was a great leveller. It respected neither pennon nor pedigree. It was a mighty agency in promoting equality by putting all classes on the same plane in the arena of arms. It brought an end to the robber barons by placing in the hands of sovereign and people a weapon before which castle walls crumbled, and compared with which the lance was but a toy.

Much has been said about gunpowder

having made war less terrible and sanguinary. The arguments in support of this assertion are more plausible than sound, and seem scarcely sustained by the records of the Thirty Years' War, the wars of Napoleon, in which millions perished, the Franco-German war, and our own great civil conflict. "War is cruelty, and you cannot refine it," said General Sherman to the city council of Atlanta, and he never spoke more truthfully. War is at least as destructive as before gunpowder vanished archer and armor, and spread its pall of smoke over the carnage of the battlefield.

Nevertheless, the destruction is not so brutalizing as in the old times when fighting was done with sword and battle-axe, and each encounter was a series of duels between men of different armies. In these days the soldier seldom knows whether he has killed anyone or not. Thousands may fall, but the combatants are, with rare exceptions, spared the knowledge of having sent the deadly missile which robbed a fellowman of life, and some home of father, husband or son. In this regard gunpowder has had a humane and humanizing influence.

Gunpowder has been the strong right arm of civilization in bringing new and savage countries under the power of Christianity. Firearms enabled Cortez to subdue Mexico, and Irmak to conquer Siberia

Without firearms the Pilgrims would have been helpless, and New Amsterdam would have been the grave of the thrifty settlers from Holland. The wondrous explorations at the close of the fifteenth century would have been fruitless but for the artificial lightning and thunder which carried terror to the breast of Aztec and Iroquois, which saved De Soto from angry savages, and brought the affrighted Tartars to the feet of Ivan the Terrible. It is a noteworthy fact, also, that England, which speedily took front rank as the champion of civil and religious progress, was swift to improve the use of artillery, and even in the reign of Henry VIII., had cannon of a superior standard on her vessels of war. This enabled the English to defeat the Spanish Armada, to assume the mastery of the seas, and to foster and protect the colonies planted by English exiles and adventurers.

In breaking down chivalry, gunpowder undoubtedly helped to pave the way for the Reformation. The reformers did not, as a rule, belong to the class of chivalry, and under mediæval conditions of warfare they would easily have been crushed. Armed with artillery they were able to meet their adversaries on terms that gave promise of success. Gunpowder was in more than one respect a useful ally to the Bible.

V.—VASCO DA GAMA'S VOYAGE.

Nothing but terrific heat which scorched and burned any navigator unlucky enough to come within its fatal sphere—nothing but death and annihilation was supposed in the popular mind of the fifteenth century to await the adventurer who should seek to penetrate beyond the northern coast line of Africa. As the North was bounded by darkness and eternal mountains of ice, so the South was assumed to have its barrier of fiery rays from a consuming sun, making life impossible and the world beyond impenetrable. It was a comforting belief for the Italian republics enjoying their monopoly of trade with India and nearer Asia, but not so pleasing to the hardy seamen of France and England and Portugal. Freed from anxiety for their own independence, as the power of the Moors declined in the peninsula, the Portuguese looked with wistful gaze toward those Oriental treasure-lands which had enriched the merchants of Venetia and Genoa. The vulgar belief that there was no ocean pathway around Africa was not shared by all. "The grand impulse to discovery," says Washington Irving, "was not given by chance, but was the deeply meditated effect of one master mind." This was Prince Henry, of Portugal, son of John the First, surnamed the

Avenger, and Philippa, of Lancaster, sister of Henry the Fourth, of England. Having accompanied his father into Africa, in an expedition against the Moors at Ceuta, Prince Henry received much information concerning the coast of Guinea and other regions in the interior hitherto unknown to Europeans, and conceived an idea that important discoveries were to be made by navigating along the western coast of Africa. On returning to Portugal, this idea became his ruling thought. Withdrawing from the tumult of a court to a country retreat in the Algarves, near Sagres, in the neighborhood of Cape St. Vincent, and in full view of the ocean, he drew around him men eminent in science, and prosecuted the study of those branches of knowledge connected with the maritime arts. He was an able mathematician, and made himself master of all the astronomy known to the Arabians of Spain. On studying the works of the ancients, he found what he considered abundant proofs that Africa was circumnavigable.

It was the grand idea of Prince Henry, by circumnavigating Africa to open a direct and easy route to the source of Asian commerce, to turn it in a golden tide upon his country. He was, however, before the age in thought, and had to counteract ignorance and prejudice, and to endure the delays to which vivid and penetrating minds are subjected, from the tardy co-operation of the dull and the doubtful. The navigation of the Atlantic was yet in its infancy. Mariners looked with distrust upon a boisterous expanse, which appeared to have no opposite shore, and feared to venture out of sight of the landmarks. Every bold headland and far-stretching promontory was a wall to bar their progress. They crept timorously along the Barbary shores, and thought they had accomplished a wonderful expedition when they had ventured a few degrees beyond the Straits of Gibraltar. Cape Nun was long the limit of their daring; they hesitated to double its rocky point, beaten by winds and waves, and threatening to thrust them forth upon the raging deep.*

Prince Henry established a naval college, and erected an observatory at Sagres, and he invited thither the most eminent professors of the nautical faculties; appointing as president, James, of Mallorca, a man learned in navigation, and skilled in making charts and instruments.

The effects of this establishment were soon apparent. All that was known relative to geography and navigation was gathered together and reduced to system.

---
*Washington Irving.

A vast improvement took place in maps. The compass was also brought into more general use, especially among the Portuguese, rendering the mariner more bold and venturous, by enabling him to navigate in the most gloomy day and in the darkest night. Encouraged by these advantages, and stimulated by the munificence of Prince Henry, the Portuguese marine became signalized for the hardihood of its enterprises and the extent of its discoveries. Cape Bojador was doubled; the region of the tropics penetrated and divested of its fancied terrors; the greater part of the African coast, from Cape Blanco to Cape de Verde, explored; and the Cape de Verde and Azore Islands, which lay three hundred leagues distant from the continent, were rescued from the oblivious empire of the ocean. To secure the quiet prosecution and full enjoyment of his discoveries, Henry obtained the protection of a papal bull, granting to the crown of Portugal sovereign authority over all the lands it might discover in the Atlantic, to India inclusive, with plenary indulgence to all who should die in these expeditions; at the same time menacing, with the terrors of the Church, all who should interfere in these Christian conquests.

* * * * * * *

Henry died on the thirteenth of November, 1473, without accomplishing the great object of his ambition. It was not until many years afterward that Vasco da Gama, pursuing with a Portuguese fleet the track Henry had pointed out, realized his anticipations by doubling the Cape of Good Hope, sailing along the southern coast of India, and thus opening a highway for commerce to the opulent regions of the East. On July 8, 1497, Vasco da Gama, an intrepid mariner, started from Lisbon in command of four vessels, fitted out by King Manuel, to discover the route to India. For months the little fleet sailed along the western coast of Africa, its progress attended by frightful storms and the difficulties of the enterprise multiplied by the rebellious conduct of the sailors. Da Gama sternly punished the mutineers, and at length rounded the southern extremity of Africa. At Melinda, on the eastern coast, the great navigator found a competent pilot, a native of India, who appeared to understand the astrolabe, compass and quadrant. Under the guidance of this man da Gama struck out boldly across the Indian Ocean and arrived at Calicut in India, May 20, 1498.

This was the beginning of Portuguese, and, indeed, of European empire in India. It was the beginning of the maritime greatness of Holland and England, as well as of

Portugal. Vasco da Gama's expedition opened the gateway of the Orient to the maritime nations of western Europe, and brought the rich and vast regions of Asia into direct communication with the more progressive nations of Europe. It was the turning point in history which led to the foundation of England's great Indian empire, to the discovery of the Australian Continent and ultimately to the opening of Japan and China to western intercourse and association. It is not to be forgotten that da Gama's expedition was the realization of the dream which inspired the voyage of Columbus, and that, from the standpoint of that day Columbus failed in endeavoring to accomplish that which da Gama successfully achieved. Columbus discovered America; da Gama uncovered southern Africa and Asia. It may be questioned even now whether the achievement of Columbus was as important in its consequences as that of da Gama. At the same time there is to be considered, in judging the comparative merits of the two men, that Columbus conceived and planned and carried out his own mighty adventure, while da Gama carried out a scheme conceived and planned by others.

VI.—FIRST VOYAGE OF COLUMBUS.

Columbus! What mighty thoughts are crowded in the name of him who lifted the veil of ages from a virgin world! No other great achievement in history was so signally the work of one man and one mind as the discovery of America. To Columbus is due all the credit and fame of that discovery, however honorable and creditable in others the fact that they dimly discerned the magnitude of his undertaking and gave him the assistance without which he could not have succeeded. No life—not even that of Washington—is so replete with lessons of encouragement for high and noble endeavor through difficulties and against obstacles that might seem to be insuperable. Men may dispute as to where the bones of Columbus rest, but there can be no dispute as to the monument which marks his fame —it is the Continent of America.

In these days when much is being written—and much of it probably untrue—about the early struggles of great men, the disappointments and privations which Columbus endured so manfully and so patiently have a renewed and pathetic interest. We perceive that, like many others of the world's heroes, he succeeded because he deserved to succeed; because he had the will, the energy, the indomitable resolution which not only deserved but commanded success. Columbus would doubtless have succeeded even had Spain rejected him; the genius which won the attention and confidence of Isabella would surely not always have met with repulse at the hands of those who controlled the means necessary to make that genius fruitful.

* * * * * * * * *

The chief crisis in the career of Columbus was that which ended in the determination of Queen Isabella to support his enterprise. The queen had been persuaded by her priestly adviser, Fernando de Talavera, that it would be 'degrading to her dignity to grant the terms demanded by Columbus, to the effect that he should be invested with the titles and privileges of admiral and viceroy over the countries he should discover, with one-tenth of all gains, either by trade or conquest. Columbus refused to abate his conditions, and the negotiations were broken off.

"It is impossible not to admire the great constancy of purpose and loftiness of spirit displayed by Columbus, ever since he had conceived the sublime idea of his discovery. More than eighteen years had elapsed since his correspondence with Paulo Toscanelli, of Florence, wherein he had announced his design. The greatest part of that time had been consumed in applications at various courts. During that period, what poverty, neglect, ridicule, contumely, and disappointment had he not suffered! Nothing, however, could shake his perseverance, nor make him descend to terms which he considered beneath the dignity of his enterprise. In all his negotiations he forgot his present obscurity; he forgot his present indigence; his ardent imagination realized the magnitude of his contemplated discoveries, and he felt himself negotiating about empire."*

Though so large a portion of his life had worn away in fruitless solicitings; though there was no certainty that the same weary career was not to be entered upon at any other court; yet so indignant was he at the repeated disappointments he had experienced in Spain, that he determined to abandon it forever, rather than compromise his demands. Taking leave of his friends, therefore, he mounted his mule, and sallied forth from Santa Fe in the beginning of February, 1492, on his way to Cordova, whence he intended to depart immediately for France.

When the few friends who were zealous believers in the theory of Columbus saw him really on the point of abandoning the

---

*Washington Irving.

country, they were filled with distress, considering his departure an irreparable loss to the nation. Among the number was Luis de St. Angel, receiver of the ecclesiastical revenues in Aragon. Determined if possible to avert the evil, he obtained an immediate audience of the queen, accompanied by Alonzo de Quintanilla. The exigency of the moment gave him courage and eloquence. He did not confine himself to entreaties, but almost mingled reproaches, expressing astonishment that a queen who had evinced the spirit to undertake so many great and perilous enterprises, should hesitate at one where the loss could be so trifling, while the gain might be incalculable. He reminded her how much might be done for the glory of God, the exaltation of the Church, and the extension of her own power and dominion. What cause of regret to herself, of triumph to her enemies, of sorrow to her friends, should this enterprise, thus rejected by her, be accomplished by some other power! He reminded her what fame and dominion other princes had acquired by their discoveries; here was an opportunity to surpass them all.

St. Angel entreated her majesty not to be misled by the assertions of learned men, that the project was the dream of a visionary. He vindicated the judgment of Columbus, and the soundness and practicability of his plans. Neither would even his failure reflect discredit upon the crown. It was worth the trouble and expense to clear up even a doubt upon a matter of such importance, for it belonged to enlightened and magnanimous princes to investigate questions of the kind, and to explore the wonders and secrets of the universe. He stated the liberal offer of Columbus to bear an eighth of the expense, and informed her that all the requisites for this great enterprise consisted but of two vessels and about three thousand crowns.

These and many more arguments were urged with that persuasive power which honest zeal imparts, and it is said the Marchioness of Moya, who was present, exerted her eloquence to persuade the queen. The generous spirit of Isabella was enkindled. It seemed as if, for the first time, the subject broke upon her mind in its real grandeur, and she declared her resolution to undertake the enterprise.

There was still a moment's hesitation. The king looked coldly on the affair, and the royal finances were absolutely drained by the war. Some time must be given to replenish them. How could she draw on an exhausted treasury for a measure to which the king was adverse! St. Angel watched this suspense with trembling anxiety. The next moment reassured him.

With an enthusiasm worthy of herself and of the cause, Isabella exclaimed, "I undertake the enterprise for my own crown of Castile, and will pledge my jewels to raise the necessary funds." This was the proudest moment in the life of Isabella; it stamped her renown forever as the patroness of the discovery of the New World.

St. Angel, eager to secure this noble impulse, assured her majesty that there would be no need of pledging her jewels, as he was ready to advance the necessary funds. His offer was gladly accepted; the funds easily came from the coffers of Aragon; seventeen thousand florins were advanced by the accountant of St. Angel out of the treasury of King Ferdinand. That prudent monarch, however, took care to have his kingdom indemnified some few years afterward; for in remuneration of this loan, a part of the first gold brought by Columbus from the New World was employed in gilding the vaults and ceilings of the royal saloon in the grand palace of Saragoza, in Aragon, anciently the Aljaferia, or abode of the Moorish kings.

Columbus had pursued his lonely journey across the Vega and reached the bridge of Pinos, about two leagues from Granada, at the foot of the mountain of Elvira, a pass famous in the Moorish wars for many a desperate encounter between the Christians and infidels. Here he was overtaken by a courier from the queen, spurring in all speed, who summoned him to return to Santa Fe. He hesitated for a moment, being loathe to subject himself again to the delays and equivocations of the court; when informed, however, of the sudden zeal for the enterprise excited in the mind of the queen, and the positive promise she had given to undertake it, he no longer felt a doubt, but, turning the reins of his mule, hastened back with joyful alacrity to Santa Fe.

On arriving at Santa Fe, Columbus had an immediate audience of the queen, and the benignity with which she received him atoned for all past neglect. Through deference to the zeal she thus suddenly displayed, the king yielded his tardy concurrence, but Isabella was the soul of this grand enterprise. She was prompted by lofty and generous enthusiasm, while the king proved cold and calculating in this as in all his other undertakings.

The capitulations were signed by Ferdinand and Isabella, at the city of Santa Fe, in the Vega or plain of Granada, on the seventeenth of April, 1492. A letter of privilege, or commission to Columbus, of similar purport, was drawn out in form, and issued by the sovereigns in the city of Granada, on the thirtieth of the same month.

In this, the dignities and prerogatives of viceroy and governor were made hereditary in his family; and he and his heirs were authorized to prefix the title of Don to their names; a distinction accorded in those days only to persons of rank and estate, though it has since lost all value, from being universally used in Spain.

All the royal documents issued on this occasion bore equally the signatures of Ferdinand and Isabella, but her separate crown of Castile defrayed all the expense; and, during her life, few persons, except Castilians, were permitted to establish themselves in the new territories.

The port of Palos was fixed upon as the place where the armament was to be fitted out, Columbus calculating, no doubt, on the co-operation of Martin Alonzo Pinzon, resident there, and on the assistance of his zealous friend, the prior of the convent La Rabida. Before going into the business details of this great enterprise, it is due to the character of the illustrious man who conceived and conducted it, most especially to notice the elevated, even though visionary, spirit by which he was actuated. One of his principal objects was undoubtedly the propagation of the Christian faith. He expected to arrive at the extremity of Asia, and to open a direct and easy communication with the vast and magnificent empire

of the Grand Khan. The conversion of
that heathen potentate had, in former times,
been a favorite aim of Roman pontiffs and
pious sovereigns, and various missions had
been sent to the remote regions of the East
for that purpose. Columbus now considered himself about to effect this great work;
to spread the light of revelation to the very
ends of the earth, and thus to be the instrument of accomplishing one of the sublime predictions of Holy Writ.

* * * * * * *

The difficulties of Columbus did not end
with his success in engaging the Spanish
sovereigns as patrons and allies in his enterprise. Weeks elapsed without a vessel being procured. Further mandates were
therefore issued by the sovereigns, ordering
the magistrates of the coast of Andalusia to
press into the service any vessels they might
think proper, belonging to Spanish subjects,
and to oblige the masters and crew to sail
with Columbus in whatever direction he
should be sent by royal command. Juan de
Penalosa, an officer of the royal household,
was sent to see that this order was properly
complied with, receiving two hundred maravedis a day as long as he was occupied in
the business, which sum, together with
other penalties expressed in the mandate,
was to be exacted from such as should be

disobedient and delinquent. This letter was acted upon by Columbus in Palos and the neighboring town of Moguer, but apparently with as little success as the preceding. The communities of those places were thrown into complete confusion; tumults took place; but nothing of consequence was effected. At length Martin Alonzo Pinzon stepped forward, with his brother Vicente Yanez Pinzon, both navigators of great courage and ability, owners of vessels, and having seamen in their employ. They were related, also, to many of the seafaring inhabitants of Palos and Moguer, and had great influence throughout the neighborhood. They engaged to sail on the expedition, and furnished one of the vessels required. Others, with their owners and crews, were pressed into the service by the magistrates under the arbitrary mandate of the sovereigns.

During the equipment of the vessels, troubles and difficulties arose among the seamen who had been compelled to embark. These were fomented and kept up by Gomez Rascon and Christoval Quintero, owners of the Pinta, one of the ships pressed into service. All kinds of obstacles were thrown in the way, by these people and their friends, to retard or defeat the voyage. The calkers employed upon the vessels did their work in a careless and imperfect manner, and on being commanded to do it over again absconded. Some of the seamen who had enlisted willingly repented of their hardihood, or were dissuaded by their relatives, and sought to retract; others deserted and concealed themselves. Everything had to be effected by the most harsh and arbitrary measures, and in defiance of popular prejudice and opposition.

The influence and example of the Pinzons had a great effect in allaying this opposition, and inducing many of their friends and relatives to embark. It is supposed that they had furnished Columbus with funds to pay the eighth part of the expense which he was bound to advance. It is also said that Martin Alonzo Pinzon was to divide with him his share of the profits. As no immediate profit, however, resulted from this expedition, no claim of the kind was ever brought forward. It is certain, however, that the assistance of the Pinzons was all-important, if not indispensable, in fitting out and launching the expedition.

After the great difficulties made by various courts in patronizing this enterprise, it is surprising how inconsiderable an armament was required. It is evident that Columbus had reduced his requisitions to the narrowest limits, lest any great expense should cause impediment. Three small vessels were apparently all that he requested. Two of them were light barks, called caravels, not superior to river and coasting craft of more modern days. Representations of this class of vessels exist in old prints and paintings. They are delineated as open, and without deck in the centre, but built up high at the prow and stern, with forecastles and cabins for the accommodation of the crew. Peter Martyr, the learned contemporary of Columbus, says that only one of the three vessels was decked.

* * * * * * *

Columbus sailed from Palos on Friday, the third of August, 1492. On losing sight of this last trace of land, the hearts of the crews failed them. They seemed literally to have taken leave of the world. Behind them was everything dear to the heart of man; country, family, friends, life itself; before them everything was chaos, mystery and peril. In the perturbation of the moment, they despaired of ever more seeing their homes. Many of the rugged seamen shed tears, and some broke into loud lamentations. The admiral tried in every way to soothe their distress, and to inspire them with his own glorious anticipations. He described to them the magnificent countries to which he was about to conduct them; the islands of the Indian seas teeming with gold and precious stones; the regions of Mangi and Cathay, with their cities of unrivaled wealth and splendor. He promised them land and riches, and everything that could arouse their cupidity or inflame their imaginations, nor were these promises made for the purposes of mere deception; he certainly believed that he should realize them all.

He now issued orders to the commanders of the other vessels, that, in the event of separation by any accident, they should continue directly westward; but that after sailing seven hundred leagues, they should lay by from midnight until daylight, as at about that distance he confidently expected to find land. In the meantime, as he thought it possible he might not discover land within the distance thus assigned, and as he foresaw that the vague terrors already awakened among the seamen would increase with the space which intervened between them and their homes, he commenced a stratagem which he continued throughout the voyage. He kept two reckonings; one correct, in which the true way of the ship was noted, and which was retained in secret for his own government; in the other, which was open to general inspection, a number of leagues was daily subtracted from the sailing of the ship, so that the crews were kept in ignorance of the real distance they had advanced.

For more than two months Columbus sailed over the unknown ocean, quieting as best he could the fears of his crew, who were about to break out in open mutiny when two signs of land fortunately became so convincing as not to admit of doubt. At length land was clearly seen. The great mystery of the ocean was revealed. His theory, which had been the scoff of sages, was triumphantly established; he had secured to himself a glory durable as the world itself. It is difficult to conceive the feelings of such a man at such a moment; or the conjectures which must have thronged upon his mind, as to the land before him, covered with darkness. That it was fruitful, was evident from the vegetables which floated from its shores. He thought, too, that he perceived the fragrance of aromatic groves. The moving light he had beheld proved it the residence of man. But what were its inhabitants? Were they like those of the other parts of the globe; or were they some strange and monstrous race, such as the imagination was prone in those times to give to all remote and unknown regions? Had he come upon some wild island far in the Indian sea; or was this the famed Cipango itself, the object of his golden fancies? A thousand speculations of the kind must have swarmed upon him, as, with his anxious crews, he waited for the night to pass away, wondering whether the morning light would reveal a savage wilderness, or dawn upon spicy groves, and glittering fanes, and gilded cities, and all the splendor of Oriental civilization.*

* * * * * * *

The immediate effect of the discovery of America by Columbus was to build up the power of Spain. It aroused also the ambition of England, of France and of Holland, and these countries soon disputed with Spain the empire of the New World. North America passed under the rule of the English-speaking races. While Spanish America sank into a volcanic torpor from which it can hardly be said to have emerged, the part of the continent controlled by men chiefly of Teutonic blood has become a highly civilized and most powerful nation, the palladium of popular institutions, and the pillar of light for those of the human race still wandering in the desert of superstition and despotism.

Spanish America has exerted hardly more influence on the affairs of the world than the benighted nations of Africa. Its

---
*Washington Irving.

greatness is yet to come, and that greatness will be, in all human probability, under English speaking auspices, with the United States as the guardian and guide of American liberty.

VII.—SPAIN'S EXPULSION OF THE JEWS.

When it is recalled that the power of Spain in the sixteenth century overshadowed Europe, while known America was a series of Spanish vice-royalties, and the wealth of the Spanish monarchy was apparently unlimited, it may be imagined what Spain could have been with the friendly guidance and assistance of the race of Disraeli and the Rothschilds. Had Spain protected the Jews instead of seeking to destroy them, Madrid might have been the rallying point and Spain the beneficiary of the most talented minds of Hebrew origin, and the Spanish dominion have been established on an enduring foundation. It is impossible to believe that Jewish financiers would have permitted Spain to go on in the course of ruinous prodigality which has left her scarce anything but Spanish poverty and pride, or that Jewish statesmen would have committed the blunders which have reduced the once powerful empire to a low place in the second rank of nations. The fortunate experience with the Jews of England and other countries which have treated them well, is the best proof of Spanish folly in the expulsion and attempted extermination of the most brilliant portion of the Jewish race, of Israelites who loved Spain as their native and ancestral land, and who would willingly have devoted their abilities to building up the power and guarding the welfare of the Spanish monarchy.

The expulsion of the Jews was a suicidal act. Retribution was not slow in overtaking the bigoted dynasty responsible for the crime; the decline of Spain has been gradual, but without interruption. Battered and plundered by the English, overrun by the French, and bankrupted in its efforts to retain the remnants of its once extensive colonial empire, Spain is to-day a mendicant at the feet of members of the very race that it so infamously persecuted.

* * * * * * *

The expulsion of the Jews from the Iberian peninsula, as a result of the cruel decree issued by Ferdinand and Isabella from their court, at Santa Fe, in the same year as the discovery of America, was, therefore, an important turning point in European history. It planted the seed of decline in the very foundation of Spain's magnificent empire, and it dispersed to more tolerant regions of Europe that bright, fervid, wealth-promoting and art-loving genius which made the Jews of Moorish Spain the very leaders of their race. The

Spanish Jews included philosophers, poets and sages, men versed alike in the learning of the ancients and the science of later centuries. Some of the most valuable classics were preserved in their Arabian translations, and to them we are indebted for works of great merit that would otherwise have been lost to the modern world. The Christian kings of that country, influenced no doubt by the example of the Moors, treated the Jews with favor, until the conquest of Granada left Castile and Aragon without a rival power of the Moslem faith in the peninsula. The year which witnessed the discovery of America witnessed the monstrous edict which crushed at one blow the Spanish Jews, and brought to poverty, ruin, and in many instances a miserable death, the most peaceable, prosperous and industrious subjects of Ferdinand and Isabella. The number driven from Spain in consequence of this decree has been estimated at from 300,000 to 800,000. It is regarded in Jewish history as a calamity as great as the destruction of Jerusalem, for indeed Spain had become to the Jews another Land of Promise.

The terror and dismay which overwhelmed the Spanish Jews can scarcely be imagined. Wailing and lamentation pervaded every dwelling, and resounded in every synagogue. Only two resources were left to those who were unwilling to abjure the religion of their forefathers. One was to escape into Portugal; the other, to flee to Morocco and other countries, where the followers of Mahomet, more Christian in feeling than the professed followers of Christ, would afford them an asylum and protection.

The scenes which occurred among those who preferred to escape entirely beyond the limits of the Roman Catholic countries, were piteous indeed. It happened that many of the ships which contained the emigrants were too heavily laden, and sank after setting sail. Other ships are recorded to have taken fire, and been lost amid all the horrors of a conflagration at sea. In many vessels diseases broke out, which carried off immense numbers of the fugitives. Several captains of vessels ordered all their Jewish passengers to be slain as the cause of the misfortunes which overtook their ships. Many perished by a violent storm which swept the deep and drove their vessels on the rocks. A famine is said to have prevailed in Morocco at the time the survivors landed, and a vast number perished of hunger; yet of the survivors, it is said that on the Friday they gathered what herbs and roots the land afforded, that they might keep the ensuing Sabbath according to their law. A large number were sold by the captains of vessels as slaves to the inhabitants of Barbary, because they were unable to comply with exorbitant demands for passage-money. It is stated by Christian writers that as many as thirty thousand Jews perished in this exodus.

* * * * * * *

In Portugal the Jews were for some time treated with tolerance and even with encouragement until King Manuel, in 1496, issued an edict banishing them from his dominions, and at the same time ordered that they should be deprived of all their children under fourteen years of age. When the Jews became victims of this new persecution they were overwhelmed with despair, and many committed suicide. Some abjured their faith, others fled to foreign countries, a large number finding refuge in France, where they received protection, and became prosperous in commerce. Many of the exiled Jews found homes in Holland, where they were received with hospitality by their brethren and with tolerance by the people, and it is unnecessary to say where lay the sympathies of these Jews and their descendants when the time came for the revolt of the Dutch against the tyranny of Spain.

A multitude of the refugees driven from one land to another, sought asylum in what might be called the neutral ground between the Eastern and Western churches. In Poland the exiled Jews became an important and influential element, filling the void between a prodigal and proud aristocracy and a servile and down-trodden peasantry. They were the mercantile and trading class in a nation which had no traders and merchants of its own. In Germany the Jews were treated, after the fifteenth century, with comparative humanity, and while the reformers did not look upon them with favor, they did not assail them as enemies. The Jew in Protestant countries inevitably shared in the advantages which attended the growth of soul independence, and even the very fury of religious strife was favorable to him in that the contestants did not regard him with the same hatred that they felt toward each other.

* * * * * * *

In prosperity, as in adversity, the Jews clung with tenacity to their ancient creed. They were as true to their faith on the banks of the Vistula as when, on the Euphrates, they sang with tears of distant Palestine:

"By the rivers of Babylon there we sat down; yea we wept when we remembered Zion. We hanged our harps upon the willows in the midst thereof.

"For there they that carried us away

captive required of us a song, and they that wasted us, mirth. Sing us of the songs of Zion.

"How shall we sing the Lord's song in a strange land?

"If I forget thee, O Jerusalem, may my right hand forget her cunning.

"If I do not remember thee, let my tongue cleave to the roof of my mouth; if I prefer not Jerusalem above my chief joy."

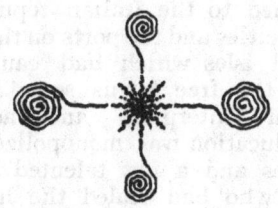

VIII.—THE REFORMATION.

Reader, try to imagine yourself in the little world of that day when Luther posted his theses on the gates of the church at Wittenberg—a world bounded on the east by Muscovy and India, on the north by the midnight sun, on the west by the new continent, discovered, but unexplored, and on the south by the African desert. Small as was the world, few people knew much about it outside of their own vicinity. Traveling was slow and difficult, and often dangerous, and the man who had visited another country than his own was regarded with wonder, if not with veneration. Foreign commerce was confined to the Italian republics, the Hanseatic cities and the ports on the western coasts and isles which had caught from Italy and the free towns some breath of commercial enterprise and adventure. Higher education was monopolized by the universities and a few talented men like Erasmus, who had scaled the heights of knowledge against difficulties almost insurmountable, and were turning the searchlight of intelligence on the phantoms of superstition. "As soon as I get money," said Erasmus, when he was penniless and in rags, "I will buy first Greek books and then clothes." The spirit which spoke in this utterance ploughed the domain of scholarship for the seeds of the Reformation.

The rudiments of learning as distinct from religious training, which are free to all in the present age in nearly every civilized country, were taught to the common people only in the burgher schools.* These schools were secular in origin and aim, and the instruction was given in municipal buildings and other structures owned or occupied by the civic authorities. The teachers were generally connected with the Church, but the schools were not ecclesiastical, and even as early as the fourteenth century, there was, it appears, some clashing on the question of secular as distinguished from religious teaching in the burgher schools.† It is noteworthy, and perhaps significant, that the first building for use solely as a public school—that is, the first schoolhouse —was built in the republican city of Berne in 1481. These burgher schools gave the people that knowledge of reading and writing necessary for intelligent study of the religious and political problems soon to be

---

*Even the better class of citizens were not always able to read and write The father of Shakespeare was an alderman, but unable to write his own name, a cross remaining as his signature in the records of the town of Stratford-on-Avon.

†As early as 1329 the citizens of Frankfort-on-the-Oden resisted their ecclesiastical superiors They remained twenty eight years without masses, baptisms, marriage or funeral rites.—*Merle D'Aubigné*

submitted to the thought and conscience of educated mankind.

Outside the cities the clergy had complete charge of education. The parish schools were drill-rooms of the church. The priests and monks taught the peasantry just enough to enable them to attend to their religious duties, and not enough to arouse a spirit of doubt and inquiry; and the simple country folk thought themselves bound to accept with unquestioning faith whatsoever they were told by their religious monitors. Neither in religion nor politics had the common people—according to the prevalent belief of that age—any right to independent preference, and it is interesting to note that this view was accepted as a matter of course by Protestants as well as Catholics.*

The State and Church were closely connected, and it was sometimes difficult to tell whether Rome or the secular head of the State had the stronger claim to allegiance. This temporal power was a cause of weakness as well as strength to the Church. The princes of northern and western Europe were rarely so wrapped up

---

*In the Diet of Augsburg in 1555, which secured for a time the religious peace of Germany, it was provided that every prince should be allowed to choose between the Catholic religion and the "Augsburg Confession," and the belief thus adopted by the prince was to be that of his people. It was not until the seventeenth century that religious toleration was more than a transient dream.

in religion as not to be jealous of the encroachments of Rome, and one of the most potent impulses of the Reformation was the desire of secular rulers to be sovereigns in fact as well as in name. Indeed, but for this feeling on the part of sovereign princes in Germany, in England, in Scandinavia, Luther and his supporters might have perished like Huss and Savonarola. Self-interest is always a powerful prick to conscience, and Henry and Frederick and Vasa were swift to see in Luther and his teachings a bulwark of their sovereignty against the assumptions of Rome. The very ignorance in which the masses had been kept under ecclesiastical tutelage made it easier for the people to be molded to the new convictions of their secular lieges.

* * * * * *

The people who could read were, therefore, already reading and thinking when Tetzel, whether innocent or guilty of the graver charges against him, caused widespread scandal and indignation by the sale of indulgences. Tetzel's formal instructions from his ecclesiastical superiors did not permit him to go to the extremes to which he appears to have resorted in order to procure money for ecclesiastical uses, but the popular mind could not draw any nice distinction, and it is not strange that while

the ignorant multitude was shocked by the
unseemly exhibition, the learned and pious
were grievously disturbed.

Suddenly, while all Germany is in ferment over Tetzel and his money-box, comes
the word that a monk at Wittenberg has
boldly declared that salvation cannot be
bought, that the pope cannot open for a
price the Kingdom of Heaven!

Men cluster in the market place, and
talk of the wondrous report; they whisper
it one to another at the gate of the church;
they haste with it to their friends—and
never had news traveled so rapidly from
hamlet to hamlet, from city to city, from
court to court, throughout Christendom.
A monk cried "Halt!" to the pope—a "contemptible monk," as Cardinal Cajetan called
him, had placed himself in opposition to all
the power of Rome. No wonder that the
pope himself did not at first perceive the
meaning of the theses of Wittenberg, and
Leo advised that Luther should not be
molested. The posting of the theses of
Wittenberg was the greatest turning point
in modern history; it was a declaration of
religious independence for Teutonic nations
at least, and it was largely instrumental in
effecting a reformation in the Roman
Church itself.

* * * * * * *

Luther himself had no idea of the scope and meaning of his Wittenberg declaration.

It was a custom of the universities, as Professor George Burton Adams points out, for a teacher who had views which he wished to publish and uphold, to post up a statement of his views as a declaration that he was prepared to defend them against all comers. Luther's honest soul was aroused in common with many others by the excesses of Tetzel, and in declaring his mind on indulgences and the abuses connected with them, he had no thought of the tremendous consequences to flow from his act. He probably expected some ecclesiastical champion of Tetzel and his methods to step forward and have a discussion with him, and that there the matter would end, so far as he was concerned.

But the people were ready for just such an awakening. Clear and Christlike as the preaching of Paul, sounded Luther's assertion that "Remission of sins and eternal life are not to be purchased by money." It was a challenge that Rome could not ignore, however secure the Roman pontiff may have felt himself in his acknowledged supremacy over the Christian world. It was a challenge echoed from heart to heart from tongue to tongue throughout Germany and France and Italy, England and Scotland, and distant Scandinavia.

Luther, astounded at the effect of his theses, could not have withdrawn from the conflict, even had he so willed. He was hurried on, as he himself declared, by a force beyond his control, and was soon at open war with the Church within whose pale he found it impossible to remain. The theses were followed not long after by Luther's address to the "Christian nobles of Germany," and his treatise on "The Babylonish Captivity of the Church," which contained, as Ranke says, "the kernel of the whole Reformation." Then came the papal bull, and then began the great struggle which, in one form or another lasted, with intervals of unquiet peace, until the present century, and the echo of which has been heard in Germany even in our own generation in the conflict between Bismarck and the Roman hierarchy.

* * * * * * *

At first it was a question whether Protestantism could survive the hostility of the powerful emperor, Charles V., of Germany and Spain. Charles was a most devoted adherent of the Church, and he employed the strength and resources of his empire in endeavoring to crush the Reformers. The latter banded together for self-defence. The League of Schmalkald included nine

Protestant princes and twelve imperial cities, and was subsequently joined by five other princes and ten imperial cities. The elector of Saxony and the landgrave of Hesse were appointed to manage its affairs. The object of the alliance, which included northern Germany, Denmark, Saxony and Wurtemberg, and portions of Bavaria and Switzerland, was the common defence of the Protestant States against imperial aggression and oppression. Luther himself drew up two "Articles of Schmalkald," setting forth the religious principles and claims of the League.

The Protestants were not as successful in the field as they ought to have been, in view of the energies and resources at their command, and had they been alone in dealing with the emperor, he would probably have subdued them. Fortunately, however, for the cause of religious liberty and progress, the attacks upon Charles by King Francis I., of France—himself, however, a most cruel and narrow-minded persecutor—and Solyman, the Magnificent, of Turkey, greatly aided the German Protestants in resisting the power of the emperor. It is an interesting fact that even the pope of Rome was for a time arrayed with the enemies of the prince, who professed to be the zealous champion of the Church, the supreme pontiff apparently regarding the temporal schemes of Charles as more menacing to papal aggrandizement than the efforts of the Reformers. While Charles was no doubt a sincere Catholic, he showed that streak of hypocrisy which seems inseparable from bigotry in his character, by keeping the pope a prisoner, made such by his own express orders, while at the same time causing prayers to be offered up for the pontiff's liberation. Notwithstanding the disastrous defeat of the League forces at Muhlberg, the emperor, pressed more than ever by external enemies, was at length obliged to concede the demands of his Protestant subjects, and to acknowledge their right to the free exercise of their religion within the States governed by the Reformers.

* * * * * * *

In England, also, the revolt against the Roman creed and supremacy received powerful impulse from causes not directly associated with questions of conscience or dogma. In England, for the first time in centuries, the king was an absolute monarch. The nobility had been almost extirpated in the Wars of the Roses, and those that remained were too weak to defy the crown, and in many cases too impoverished to be independent of the royal bounty. Under Henry VI., Sir John Fortescue had declared that "a king of England cannot at his pleasure make any alteration in the laws of the land. . . . He is appointed to protect his subjects in their lives, properties and laws; for this very end and purpose he has the delegation of power from the people, and he has no just claim to any other power but this." A similar assertion under Henry VIII. would have brought the person uttering it to the block.

The parliament was a parliament only in name, and merely registered the wishes of the king. Indeed parliament was useful to the monarch, without being in any sense a restraint upon him, for while it fulfilled his dictates with Oriental subserviency, it relieved him of the odium of putting his more odious caprices into the form of law. The Tudor kings were czars, without a czar's responsibility.

It was to the most absolute of English monarchs, Henry VIII., that the desire came to divorce his Spanish wife, Katharine, and to wed an English lady of good family, Anne Boleyn. The marriage of Henry and Katharine had been a contract of policy, not of love. The couple probably never cared much for each other, although Katharine was a true wife. Her stately virtue and chilling dignity alienated a husband whose affections, as history shows, were too readily inclined to stray, and he sought in more pleasing companionship the happiness which the Spanish princess seemed unable to bestow. Henry's great minister, Cardinal Wolsey, earnestly supported the king's application to Rome for a divorce, with the hope and expectation that Henry would marry a daughter of France. When the cardinal learned that the object of Henry's passion was a young woman, not of princely parentage, and whose friends were inclined to the opinions proclaimed at Wittenberg, and already planted in England, he became lukewarm, and sought to delay and obstruct the divorce proceedings.*

Even had Wolsey stood sincerely by his sovereign and Anne Boleyn, it is not probable that Pope Clement would have granted a divorce and thereby have deeply offended the sovereign of Germany and Spain, to whose family Katharine belonged. It was one thing for the pope to oppose the territorial designs of the Emperor Charles; it would have been quite another and far more serious matter to have branded a daughter of Aragon as having been unlawfully wedded to the English king, and her child as not entitled to her father's crown.

---

*The movement originated by Wycliffe, the greatest of the "Reformers before the Reformation," may be said to have been extinguished long before the dispute between Henry VIII. and the pope. Nevertheless the spirit which gave Wycliffe the support for a time of king and nation against the pretensions of Rome never was extinguished in England. It existed before Wycliffe and it survived him.

The abolition of papal authority in England was the direct result of the pope's refusal to declare the marriage to Katharine invalid, and from the hour of that declaration England was lost to Rome. England did not become a Protestant country at once; under Henry it remained virtually Catholic, save as to papal supremacy. It took many years for the Protestant faith to become established as the creed of the people as well as the law of the land. The nation marched steadily forward, however, in the path of the Reformation, and even the reign of Mary, Katharine's daughter, was hardly a pause in its progress.

* * * * * * *

In Scotland reformation sprang from the people, and was the fruit of deep and earnest religious convictions. The Church and crown were at first united in striving to extinguish the flame of revived Christianity, but the efforts of both were vain against a preacher like Knox, sustained by a powerful element in the nobility, and the large majority of the lower classes. Scotland became a bulwark of the new religion in its more radical form, and was the scene for many years of unhappy strife between the supporters of Episcopacy and the adherents of that confession of faith to which James VI. subscribed in his youth.

* * * * * * *

Perhaps the most astonishing work of the Reformation was its effect upon the people of the Netherlands. Cautious, peace-loving and commercial, the men and women of the provinces, afterward known as the Dutch Republic, would hardly have been suspected of the heroic qualities which they displayed in their struggle with Spain. Only the most exalted motives could have evoked that wondrous spirit of patriotism and religious enthusiasm which made the Netherlands an arena of one of the greatest conflicts of modern times, which defied torture at the stake and death on the battlefield, and halted the hordes of Alva at the western gate of Germany. A new nation sprang into being, destined to take no unimportant part in planting in the newly discovered world the principles of human progress and liberty, and counteracting in the continent which Spain had discovered the extension of Spanish bigotry and misrule. The story of the Dutch Republic is a chapter of the Reformation, and could never have been written but for the Reformation. The torch of liberty in the Netherlands was lighted in the flame of Wittenberg.

* * * * * * *

The same year in which Luther published his address "to the Christian nobles of Germany," witnessed the "blood-bath of Stock-

holm." The story is worth telling, for it
had a momentous influence on the religious
destinies of Europe. Christian II., of Denmark, was crowned king of Sweden in the
church of St. Nikolaus, at Stockholm, late
in the autumn of 1520. For three days the
feasting and rejoicing went on. The king
was in especial good humor, and kissed and
embraced many of the guests. On the
fourth day, when the festivities were at
their height, many of the first nobles of the
kingdom, together with the chief burghers
of Stockholm and some of the most distinguished prelates of the Church, were suddenly summoned into the great hall of the
palace. Here, to their utter astonishment,
a charge of heresy was raised against them,
and on this flimsy pretext the nobles and
burghers were thrown into the dungeons
of the tower, and the clergy imprisoned in
a room by themselves.

At noon of the following day the gates of
the palace were thrown open, and there
marched forth a sorrowful procession—the
best men of Sweden, surrounded by soldiers
and executioners. First came the bishops,
Vincentius and Matthias, clad in ceremonial
robes of the Church; next, senators, in
their regalia of office, followed by the
mayors and council and chief citizens of
Stockholm. They were conducted to the
great market-place hard by. Here the

soldiers formed a hollow square around the doomed men. Then a Danish councilor called upon the populace not to be alarmed at what was about to take place, since these prisoners had sinned against the Church. At this Bishop Vincentius raised his voice and cried out, "This is not true. I demand a legal trial. The king is traitor to the Swedes and God will punish him."

About six hundred of the best men of Sweden perished before the "bath of blood" came to an end. Even children were not spared. Two little boys, eight and six years of age, were beheaded, with their father, at Jonkoping. The elder son was first decapitated. When the younger saw the flowing blood dye his brother's clothes, he said to the headsman, "Dear man, don't let my shirt get all bloody like brother's, for mother will whip me if you do." This childish prattle touched the heart of even the grim headsman. Flinging away his sword, he cried, "Sooner shall my own shirt be stained with blood than I make bloody yours, my boy." The barbarous king beckoned to a more hardened butcher, who first cut off the head of the lad, and then that of the executioner, who had shown mercy.

This "blood-bath" led to the rising under Gustavus Vasa against Danish oppression. "The fate of Sweden, aye, the

outcome of the Thirty Years' War, the fate
of Europe, the salvation of the Protestant
faith, all hung upon the decision of that
fair-haired, full-bearded young Swede, as he
stood leaning on his staff on that winter's
day amid the snow in the northern forest"
—listening to the prayer of the Dalkarlar
to return and lead them against the Danes.*
Gustavus Vasa was, from the first, inclined
toward the Reformation, and ultimately
succeeded in making Lutheranism the national religion of Sweden. Gustavus
Adolphus, grandson of the founder of the
House of Vasa, undoubtedly saved Protestantism from being extinguished in Germany by the mercenaries of Austria and
the Catholic League.

* * * * * * * *

The Reformers did not overthrow the
ancient creed in France; but they gave to
that nation the heroic epoch of its history,
an epoch thrilling with self-sacrifice,
with martyrdom, with battle scenes more
brilliant than any that chivalry had presented, and with piety and purity of motive
deeper than chivalry had ever known.
The Reformation, had it succeeded, would
doubtless have prevented the French Revolution. Defeated and overcome as it was,
it deferred the Revolution by giving a

---
*"Sweden and the Swedes."—*W. W. Thomas, Jr.*

healthy tone for a time to the body politic,
and by turning the minds of men toward
the remedies which religion suggests for
the evils which afflict the State. When
Protestantism departed from France, its
place was quickly occupied by irreligious
philosophy and speculation, which clearly
pointed to a great political and social con-
vulsion as the only cure for the unspeakable
misrule of the Bourbons.

* * * * * * *

I have already said that the Reformation
was progressive. It is progressing to-day.
There has been no religious turning-point
since Wittenberg. In some respects the
Protestantism of the sixteenth century was
not different from Rome. The early reformers were opposed to Rome because they
believed Rome to be wrong, and in defending their own belief, they were just as in-
tolerant as Rome of any difference from the
creed they professed. They persecuted
Catholics and they persecuted each other.
It was more than a century before the principle of religious toleration found lodgment
in the minds of men, and it was more than
two hundred years from Wittenberg before
the dissenter from the recognized creed,
either in Protestant or Catholic countries,
ceased to be regarded and generally treated
as a foe within the political household.

And yet toleration was the inevitable and logical outcome of Luther's revolt against Rome. The right of individual judgment implied tolerance for those who conscientiously arrived at a certain belief, provided they were loyal and obedient to the civil law. If Protestants were a long time in coming to this conclusion, and in some countries have not quite arrived at it yet, it should be remembered that political circumstances narrowed the horizon of conscience, that Europe was for centuries the scene of sanguinary religious strife, and that it was only too true in those perilous times that a religious antagonist was a public enemy. To this rule the history of Great Britain presented noble exceptions, but in Germany, swept and swept again by religious wars during the sixteenth and seventeenth centuries, and desolated by armies destroying each other in the name of Him who came to bring peace and goodwill to men, a difference in creed long meant a difference in allegiance.

IX.—TRIAL OF THE SEVEN BISHOPS.

"It is indeed," says Buckle, "difficult to conceive the full amount of the impetus given to English civilization by the expulsion of the House of Stuart. Among the most immediate results, may be mentioned the limits that were set to the royal prerogative; the important steps that were taken toward religious toleration; the remarkable and permanent improvement in the administration of justice; the final abolition of a censorship over the press; and, what has not excited sufficient attention, the rapid growth of those great monetary interests by which, as we shall hereafter see, the prejudices of the superstitious classes have in no small degree been counterbalanced. These are the main characteristics of the reign of William III.; a reign often aspersed, and little understood, but of which it may be truly said, that, taking its difficulties into due consideration, it is the most successful and the most splendid recorded in the history of any country."

The Declaration by both Houses of the English Parliament, when the crown was offered to William and Mary, clearly set forth the reasons for which James the Second was dethroned. "Whereas," it was declared, "the late king, James the Second, by the assistance of divers evil counsellors, judges, and ministers, employed by him, did endeavor to subvert and extirpate the Protestant religion, and the laws and liberties of this kingdom; by assuming and exercising a power of dispensing with and suspending of laws, and the execution of laws, without consent of Parliament; by committing and prosecuting divers worthy prelates, for humbly petitioning to be excused from concurring to the said assumed power; by issuing and causing to be executed, a commission, under the great seal, for erecting a court called 'The Court of Commissioners for Ecclesiastical Causes;' by levying money for and to the use of the crown, by pretence of prerogative, for other time and in other manner than the same was granted by Parliament; by raising and keeping a standing army within the kingdom, in time of peace, without consent of Parliament, and quartering soldiers contrary to law; by causing several good subjects, being Protestants, to be disarmed, at the same time when papists were both armed and employed contrary to law; by violating of members to serve in Parliament; by prosecutions in the Court of King's Bench for matters and causes cognizable only in Parliament, and by divers other arbitrary and illegal causes; And whereas, of late years, partial, corrupt, and unqualified persons have been returned, and served on juries, and particularly divers jurors in trials for high treason, which were not freeholders; and excessive bail hath been required of persons committed in criminal cases, to elude the benefit of the laws made for the liberty of the subjects; and excessive fines have been imposed; and illegal and cruel punishments inflicted; and several grants and promises made of fines and forfeitures, before any conviction or judgment against the persons upon whom the same were to be levied; all which are utterly and directly contrary to the known laws, and statutes, and freedom of this realm.''

This Declaration, or "Bill of Rights," as it is commonly known, is the "greater charter" of the English people, the original charter also of American liberty. It affirmed the freedom of debate in parliament, the freedom of elections and the freedom of petition. It assured the subjects of the British crown against the usurpation of absolute power by royalty, and it made the throne of England a constitutional monarchy.

The Revolution of 1688 was not less decisive in its influence on the destinies of America. James II. had overturned popular government in the colonies, and at-

tempted to establish a despotic vice-royalty
in its place. With the mother country acquiescent in his tyrannical rule, the feeble
settlements in America would have been
helpless. The deliverance of England was
the deliverance of all who owed allegiance
to the English crown. It was the end of
divine right as a title to the throne; it was
the knell of the British Bourbons who had
worn so unworthily the mantle of Bruce and
of Edward.

It seems incredible that even a Stuart
should have thought of rolling back the car
of progress for over a century, restoring
the papal connection, and reviving the
arbitrary methods of government for which
James the Second's father lost his head.
James ascended the throne under the most
favorable auspices for a successful and happy
reign—barring his own determination to
abuse the power intrusted to him. The
attempt to exclude him from the succession
had failed, and the conservative sentiment
of the country was friendly to the new king.
"The magistrates of Middlesex," says
Macaulay, "thanked God for having confounded the designs of those regicides and
excluders who, not content with having
murdered one blessed monarch, were bent
on destroying the foundations of monarchy.
The city of Gloucester execrated the blood-thirsty villains who had tried to deprive

his majesty of his just inheritance. The
burgesses of Wigan assured their sovereign
that they would defend him against all
plotting Ahithophels and rebellious Absaloms. The grand jury of Suffolk expressed a hope that the parliament would
proscribe all the excluders. Many corporations pledged themselves never to return
to parliament any person who had voted
for taking away the birthright of James.
Even the capital was profoundly obsequious.
The lawyers and traders vied with each
other in servility. Inns of court and inns
of chancery sent up fervent professions of
attachment and submission. All the great
commercial societies, the East India Company, the African Company, the Turkey
Company, the Muscovia Company, the Hudson's Bay Company, the Maryland Merchants, the Jamaica Merchants, the Merchant
Adventurers, declared that they most cheerfully complied with the royal edict which
required them still to pay custom. Bristol,
the second city of the island, echoed the
voice of London. But nowhere was the
spirit of loyalty stronger than in the two
universities. Oxford declared that she
would never swerve from those religious
principles which bound her to obey the
king without any restrictions or limitations.
Cambridge condemned, in severe terms, the
violence and treachery of those turbulent

men who had maliciously endeavored to turn the stream of succession out of the ancient channel."

James proceeded to show his appreciation of all this confidence by forthwith plotting to secure absolutism for himself and to antagonize the religious faith of the vast majority of Englishmen. His misrule provoked the rebellion headed by the Duke of Monmouth, the natural son of Charles the Second, and nephew of James. The rising was poorly planned and easily defeated. It gave James an opportunity which he eagerly seized to suppress constitutional agitation and freedom of speech under the cover of punishing treason.*

* * * * * * *

---

*"It has not been generally thought that," says Macaulay, "either after the rebellion of 1715, or after the rebellion of 1745, the House of Hanover erred on the side of clemency; yet all the executions of 1715 and 1745 added together will appear to have been few indeed when compared with those which disgraced the Bloody Assizes. The number of the rebels whom Jeffreys hanged on this circuit was 320. Lonsdale says 700, and Burnet 600." In Somersetshire, "the chief seat of the rebellion, 233 prisoners were in a few days hanged, drawn and quartered. At every spot where two roads met, on every market-place, on the green of every village which had furnished Monmouth with soldiers, ironed corpses clattering in the wind, or heads and quarters stuck on poles, poisoned the air, and made the traveler sick with horror In many parishes the peasantry could not assemble in the house of God without seeing the ghastly face of a neighbor grinning at them over the porch. The Chief Justice was all himself. His spirits rose higher and higher as the work went on. He laughed, shouted, joked and swore in such a way that many thought him drunk from morning to night; but in him it was not easy to distinguish the madness produced by evil passions from the madness produced by brandy."

The terror inspired by the "Bloody Assizes" encouraged James to step still farther toward the precipice, and he now began plotting to break down the English church, with the eventual object of a reconciliation with Rome. He pretended to favor freedom of religious worship, while taking a course which, if successful, would have resulted in the enslavement of the English people, and the extension to England of the religious conditions which prevailed in France and Spain and Italy. The clergy resolutely resisted the royal decrees, and the climax was reached in the imprisonment in the Tower of the seven bishops who ventured upon a respectful remonstrance against the action of the king.

James had ordered that his declaration of indulgence should be read by the clergy in the churches immediately after divine service. A meeting of bishops was held at Lambeth Palace, and it was resolved to petition the king to recall the order. The words of the petition were, "that the great averseness found in themselves to their distributing and publishing, in all their churches, your majesty's late declaration for liberty of conscience, proceeds neither from any want of duty nor obedience to your majesty; our holy mother, the Church of England, being, both in her principles and her constant practice, unquestionably loyal, and having, to her great honor, been more than once publicly acknowledged to be so by your gracious majesty; nor yet from any want of tenderness to dissenters, in relation to whom we are willing to come to such a temper as shall be thought fit, when the matter shall be considered and settled in Parliament and Convocation; but among other considerations, from this especially, because that declaration is founded upon such a dispensing power as hath been often declared illegal in Parliament, and particularly in the years 1662 and 1672, and in the beginning of your majesty's reign; and is a matter of so great moment and consequence to the whole nation, both in Church and State, that your petitioners cannot, in common prudence, honor, or conscience, so far make themselves parties to it, as the distribution of it all over the nation, and the solemn publication of it once and again, even in God's house, and in the time of divine service, must amount to in common and reasonable construction.''

King James was deeply offended, and the bishops were arrested and committed to the Tower on the charge of having contrived, written and published a seditious libel. The excitement was intense, and the trial was watched as no State trial had been watched before. A deafening huzza from the audience welcomed the jury's verdict of acquittal, and that shout was echoed from town to town, from hamlet to hamlet throughout the land. From that day the Stuart dynasty was doomed.

All eyes were now turned to William, Prince of Orange, the husband of Mary, the Protestant daughter of King James. William was one of the ablest generals and statesmen of his time, and he promptly proceeded to collect men and arms for an expedition against his father-in-law. He also published a declaration in favor of popular rights and condemning the arbitrary government of James. The landing of William at Torbay, the flight of James, and the elevation of William and Mary to the throne need not be described here. The great turning point in English, and I may add also in American, history, was the trial of the seven bishops, which aroused the English people from the stupor of despotism, and laid fast and sure the foundation of popular sovereignty.

X.—HUTCHINSON'S WRITS OF ASSISTANCE.

"Governor Hutchinson is dead. * * *
He was born to be the cause and victim of
popular fury, outrage and conflagrations.
Descended from an ancient and honorable
family; born and educated in America;
professing all the zeal of the Congregational religion; affecting to honor the characters of the first planters of the New
World, and to vindicate the character of
America and especially of New England;
early initiated into public business; industrious and indefatigable in it; beloved
and esteemed by the people; elected and
trusted by them and their representatives;
his views opened and extended by repeated
travels in Europe; engaged in extensive
correspondence in Europe as well as in
America; favored with the crown of Great
Britain, and possessed of its honors and
emoluments—possessed of all these advantages and surrounded by all these circumstances, he was perhaps the only man in
the world who could have brought on the
controversy between Great Britain and
America in the manner and at the time it
was done, and involved the two countries
in an enmity which must end in their everlasting separation. Yet this was the char-

acter of the man, and these his memorable actions. An inextinguishable ambition and avarice, that were ever seen among his other qualities, and which grew with his growth, and strengthened with his age and experience, and at last predominated over every other passion of his heart and principle of his mind, rendered him credulous to a childish degree of everything that favored his ruling passion, and blind and deaf to everything that thwarted it to such a degree that his representations with those of his fellow-laborer, Bernard, drew on the king, ministry, parliament and nation to concert measures which will end in their reduction, and the exaltation of America.''

Such is the description by John Adams, in a letter to the President of the Congress, June 17, 1780, of the man who, as Chief Justice of Massachusetts, was instrumental in the measures which aroused the colonists to the necessity of defending their liberties, and of opposing a united front to British injustice and oppression.

When the colonists, their western bounds no longer threatened by civilized foes, their plantations flourishing and their seaport towns wealthy with the profits of a commerce carried on in contempt of imperial restrictions, began to feel and to assert that they were entitled to all the rights of freeborn Englishmen, and to the same commercial and industrial independence enjoyed by loyal subjects in England, they were surprised to learn that parliament and the English people regarded them not as freemen, but as tributaries. The colonists were themselves loyal, even up to the hour when they were compelled by stubborn tyranny to assert the right of revolution, for, to quote the language of John Adams, "it is true there always existed in the colonies a desire of independence of Parliament in the articles of internal taxation and internal policy, and a very general, if not universal opinion, that they were constitutionally entitled to it, and as general a determination to maintain and defend it. But there never existed a desire of independence of the Crown, or of general regulations of commerce for the equal and impartial benefit of all parts of the empire." "If any man," said the same great statesman, "wishes to investigate thoroughly the causes, feelings and principles of the Revolution, he must study this Act of Navigation, and the Acts of Trade, as a philosopher, a politician and a philanthropist."

When the Act of Navigation was originally passed, in the Cromwell period, it is probable that the colonies were not seriously in the minds of the people and of parliament. The act was aimed by English trading interests, at the Dutch, and was effective for the purposes intended; but within the decade that elapsed before its re-enactment under the Restoration, the colonial trade had grown with a vigor that aroused jealousy and uneasiness at home, and the Act of Navigation was soon followed, in 1663, by the first of the Acts of Trade, which provided that no supplies should be imported into any colony, except what had been actually shipped in an English port, and carried directly thence to the importing colony. This cut the colonies off from direct trade with any foreign country, and made England the depot for all necessaries or luxuries which the colonies desired, and which they could not obtain in America. Nine years later, in 1672, followed another act "for the better securing the plantation trade," which recited that the colonists had, contrary to the express letter of the aforesaid laws, brought into diverse parts of Europe great quantities of their growth, productions and manufactures, sugar, tobacco, cotton, wool and dye woods being particularly enumerated in the list, and that the trade and navigation in those commodities from one plantation to another had been greatly increased, and provided that all colonial commodities should either be shipped to England or Wales before being imported into another colony, or that a customs duty should be paid on such commodities equivalent to the cost of conveying the same to England, and thence to the colony for which they were destined. For instance, if a merchant in Rhode Island desired to sell some product of the colony of Massachusetts in New York, and to forward the same by vessel, either a bond had to be given that the commodity would be transported to England, or a duty had to be paid, in money or in goods, sufficiently onerous to protect the English merchant and ship-owner against serious colonial competition in the carrying trade.

The above act was followed up by another providing penalties for attempted violation of the customs laws. In this statute no mention was made of the plantations, and its general tenor indicated that it was intended to apply to Great Britain only, providing, as it did, for the searching of houses and dwellings for smuggled goods by virtue of a writ of assistance under the seal of His Majesty's court of exchequer. Under William the Third, who was as arbitrary a monarch toward the colonies as the second James had been, the statute was made directly applicable to the plantation trade, with the provision that "the like assistance shall be given to the said officers in the execution of their office, as by the last-mentioned act is provided for the offcers in

England." It was on the question of whether such a writ could be issued from a colonial court that James Otis made the famous speech in which he arraigned the commercial policy of England, stripped the veil of reform from the bust of the Stadtholder-King, and awakened the colonists to a throbbing sense of English oppression and of American wrongs—the oration which, in the language of John Adams, who heard it, "breathed into this nation the breath of life."

* * * * * * *

It is needless to follow the numerous Acts of Trade in their order, for they were all in a line with the accepted and established principle of that age in England, that the colonies should minister to the commercial aggrandizement of the mother country, instead of being the centres of an independent traffic, that they should be communities for the consumption of British manufactures and the feeding of British trade. New England was especially the object of English jealousy and restriction, and for reasons, as given by Sir Josiah Child, in his "New Discourse on Trade," written about the year 1677, that are creditable to the founders of those States, or after speaking of the people of Virginia and the Barbadoes as a loose vagrant sort, "vicious and destitute of means to live at home, gathered up about the streets of London or other places, and who, had there been no English foreign plantation in the world, must have come to be hanged or starved, or died untimely of those miserable diseases that proceed from want and vice, or have sold themselves as soldiers to be knocked on the head, or at best, by begging or stealing two shillings and sixpence, have made their way to Holland to become servants to the Dutch, who refuse none," he goes on to describe "a people whose frugality, industry and temperance and the happiness of whose laws and institutions do promise to themselves long life, with a wonderful increase of people, riches and power." But, after paying this probably reluctant tribute to New England virtue and industry, he frankly avows his full sympathy with the restrictive system, and adds that "there is nothing more prejudicial and in prospect more dangerous to any mother kingdom than the increase of shipping in her colonies, plantations and provinces." It is no wonder that John Adams said that he never read these authors without being set on fire, and that at last the same fire spread to every patriotic breast.

The Acts of Navigation and of Trade were not the dead letters that some superficial writers and readers have seen fit to term them. It is true that obedience was reluctant and slow, and that evasion was extensive, and it is also true, that colonial commerce flourished in spite of the restrictions; but it should be remembered that the prolonged wars in which England was engaged gave lucrative opportunities for privateering, and that even the customs duties, though intended to be virtually prohibitory, were not heavy enough to overcome the advantages which the colonists enjoyed. In Rhode Island the General Assembly asserted and maintained the right to regulate the fees of the customs officers, and, as far as was possible, the collection of the dues. The shipping of the colony rapidly increased, and in 1731 included two vessels from England, as many from Holland and the Mediterranean, and ten or twelve from the West Indies, and ten years later numbered one hundred and twenty vessels engaged in the West Indian, African, European and coasting trade. The period preceding the Revolution witnessed New England's greatest commercial prosperity, and it was in that age that Moses Brown and other enterprising merchants and shipowners laid the foundation of fortunes, a liberal share of which has been expended with illustrious munificence in monuments of learning, of art and of charity. As for the restrictions upon domestic industry they were not severely felt among a people devoted, in the country to agriculture, and in the towns to local traffic and shipping, and the American farmer who wore homespun attire, did not realize the harshness or appreciate the purpose of the statute which prohibited the export of wool or woolen manufactures. As for the Southern planter, the question of fostering domestic manufactures never entered his thoughts. He raised his tobacco and his cotton, exported them to England, and got what goods he needed there just as his descendants, in a later age, procured the manufactured necessities and luxuries of life from the depots of New England trade.*

But even if the British Parliament had never attempted to raise a revenue by taxation in the American colonies, it is probable that in time the restrictions on commerce would have led to revolution, unless rescinded. This was the opinion of the shrewd observer Du Chatelet, who, after France had surrendered her American possessions to Great Britain, said that "they (the chambers of commerce) regard everything in colonial commerce which does not turn exclusively to the benefit of the kingdom as contrary to the end for which colonies were established, and as a theft from

---
*"English Free Trade; Its Foundation, Growth and Decline." By Henry Mann

the State. To practice on these maxims is
impossible. The wants of trade are stronger
than the laws of trade. The north of
America can alone furnish supplies to its
south. This is the only point of view under
which the cession of Canada can be regarded
as a loss for France; but that cession will
one day be amply compensated, if it shall
cause in the English colonies the rebellion
and the independence which become every
day more probable and more near."

* * * * * * *

America, if not contented, was quiet under restrictive laws not stringently enforced,
and but for the measures initiated by Gren-
ville and Townshend, and approved by the
king, the parliament and the people of
England, there would, if the leading American minds of that day were sincere, have
been no insurrection in that era against
British authority. George the Third is
called a tyrant on every recurring Fourth
of July, but the nation he ruled was as
tyrannical as he, and impartial history
cannot condemn the monarch without
awarding a greater share of odium to his
people, who sustained by their pronounced
opinion and through their chosen representatives, every measure for the destruction
of the liberties of these colonies, and who
began to listen to the dictates of reason and

of humanity only when America had become the prison of thousands of England's soldiers, and thousands of others, hired Hessian and kidnaped Briton alike, had been welcomed by American freemen to graves in American soil. The measures which led to war, and the war itself, were inspired and incited by the trading classes, as well as the aristocracy of England, who expected, in the destruction of a powerful commercial and menacing industrial rival, an ample return for the blood and treasure expended in the strife. The American people recognized that the struggle was for commercial and industrial as well as for political independence, and the stand in behalf of American industry was taken long before the scattered colonies met an empire in the field of arms.

Even before peace had been made with France the king's officers in America began to enforce the revenue laws with a rigor to which the colonists had been unaccustomed. Charles Paxton, commissioner of customs in Boston, applied to the Superior Court for authority to use writs of assistance in searching for smuggled goods. These writs were warrants for the officers to search when and where they pleased and to call upon others to assist them, instead of procuring a special search warrant for some designated place. Thomas Hutchinson, chief justice, and afterward royalist governor and refugee, favored the application, which was earnestly opposed by the merchants and the people generally. "To my dying day," exclaimed James Otis, in pleading against the measure, "I will oppose with all the power and faculties God has given me, all such instruments of slavery on one hand, and of villainy on the other." Parliament had authorized the issue of the writs, however, and the custom house officers therefore had the law on their side. Writs were granted, but their enforcement was attended with so many difficulties that the customs authorities virtually gave up this attempt to encroach upon the rights of the people. The next step in provoking the colonists to revolution was the Stamp Act. The object of this enactment was to raise money for the support of British troops and the payment of salaries to certain public officers in the colonies who had depended upon the colonial treasuries for their compensation. In this there was a threefold invasion of colonial rights. Taxation without representation was contrary to a principle recognized for centuries in England, vindicated in the revolution which cost Charles I. his head, and upheld in America from the very beginning of the settlements here. Again, while British troops had been welcome as allies in battling against the French and the Indians, they were not desired as garrisons to overawe the free people of the colonies, and finally the colonial officers whom it was proposed to pay from the royal treasury would become the masters instead of servants of the people—or they would be servants only of the king. The purpose of the Stamp Act obviously was to make America the vassal of Great Britain. The act required that legal documents and commercial instruments should be written, and that newspapers should be printed, on stamped paper.

* * * * * * *

The people everywhere protested against the tyrannical action of Parliament. Samuel Adams drew up the instructions to the newly-elected representatives of Boston to use all efforts against the plan of parliamentary taxation. It was resolved "that the imposition of duties and taxes by the Parliament of Great Britain upon a people not represented in the House of Commons is irreconcilable with their rights." A committee of correspondence was appointed in Massachusetts to communicate with other colonial assemblies, and the idea of union for the common defence began to take firm hold on the public mind. Benjamin Franklin, in the Congress held at Albany in 1754 to insure the aid of the Six Nations in the war then breaking out with France, had proposed a plan of union for the colonies, with a grand council having extensive powers and a president to be appointed by the crown. The plan was not adopted. Adams had written about the same time that "the only way to keep us from setting up for ourselves is to disunite us." Everybody now began to perceive the need of union, which the great intellects of Franklin and Adams had discerned long before.

* * * * * *

The story of the American Revolution need not be told over again in these pages. The turning-point toward that tremendous struggle, with all its burden of destiny for mankind, was the issue of writs of assistance by Thomas Hutchinson, Chief Justice of Massachusetts. Hutchinson paid a bitter penalty for the wrong he had done his country. He did not live to see independence achieved, but he lived long enough to keenly feel the chill of royal displeasure and aversion, resulting from evidence which even King George could not disregard that American patriotism and endurance had been grossly undervalued and misrepresented by the so-called American loyalists.

The political effects of the American

Revolution have been almost entirely confined to the American continent. While the revolt of the Spanish-American colonies was neither inspired nor promoted from the United States, the newly-enfranchised nations adopted our institutions, in form at least. Their independence to-day of European dictation and interference is largely due to the influence on Europe of the presence of a great power in North America able to repel and rebuke European encroachment.

But when we look toward Europe we see there no sign of American influence in national politics, no disposition to adopt or imitate our American system of government. The French Revolution had no inspiration from this side of the Atlantic, and wherever the people of Europe have been admitted to a voice in public affairs, English, and not American, institutions have been copied. America is politically isolated from the rest of the world. We neither give nor take. Europe has progressed according to lines of its own; and we along lines that are distinct and separate from those of the parent continent.

The most important political effect of the American Revolution, outside of our own boundaries, has been to make England discard her policy of selfishness in dealing with her colonies. Had the American War of Independence ended differently, Canada and Australia would not, in all probability, have home rule to-day. Like Charles the Second, who did not care to go on his travels again, England has not cared to risk more revolutions by a policy of injustice and oppression. This effect of the American Revolution has been a gain not only for England and her colonies, but for mankind.

* * * * * * *

An effect of the American Revolution of vast advantage to all the world is the development of American genius under free institutions. It is a noteworthy fact that the great discoveries of the eighteenth and nineteenth centuries have had their birth in England and America, and America has full right to claim at least equal honors with the mother land. The climate of despotism is not favorable to the flower of genius; and the same may be said of a cramped colonial horizon. It is difficult to believe that a Fulton, a Morse, or an Edison would have grown to maturity in colonial soil, and we may say the same of a Watt or a Stephenson. The ozone of liberty is a healthy stimulus to inventive talent.

The American Revolution made it certain that the western hemisphere would be free from crowns and kings, that in North and South America the problem of popular self-government would be worked out under the most favorable auspices possible. The Revolution did not solve the problem; it is not solved yet; more ordeals may try the nation's courage and grit and integrity before it will be solved; but there is every reason to hope and believe that the spirit which has subdued every obstacle in the past will not be wanting in the trials to come.

XI.—THE GUILLOTINE VERSUS THE DIVINE RIGHT OF KINGS.

There is one passion in the minds of men stronger than love of liberty—it is national pride. It is a passion which has often defeated the best designed schemes of rulers and statesmen, which has sometimes retarded the progress of mankind, and maintained nationality at the cost of many advantages. It is not a passion to be despised or condemned, for it is patriotism in its crude, untempered form, and history is red-lettered with the deeds of heroism, loyalty and self-sacrifice springing from that spirit which preferred national identity with all its drawbacks to civilization and progress as gifts from an alien hand. The Edwardian conquest was a distinct benefit to Scotland, yet that fact does not diminish our admiration of Wallace and of Bruce. The majority of the Poles probably lost nothing, and many of them came under better conditions by the partition of Poland, yet Poland's brave and hopeless struggle for the restoration of a nationality whose government was in all respects the worst in Europe, evokes our deepest sympathy.

It was mainly this spirit which defeated the French Revolution and its offspring, the

First Empire, in their attempts to extend liberal institutions to other countries of Europe. And yet the French Revolution was a memorable turning-point in history, and the changes which it brought about in the institutions of the continent could not be effaced by all the efforts of the Holy Alliance. It began as a flood, violent and destructive in its course, and it swept first over France, and then over Italy and Germany and Spain and lesser countries, carrying away the ancient landmarks so swiftly and fiercely that they could never be fully restored, and leaving a political desert, studded with altars of liberty, as odious as they seemed impious to the subject people.*
The French revolutionists overthrew principalities and republics alike. There was nothing constructive in their policy. As iconoclasts, as exterminators of ancient régimes, whether of liberty or despotism, they surpassed the Goths and the Vandals.

---

* The presence and proceedings of the French in Leghorn were alike odious to the inhabitants, who found an important branch of their trade—that with England—completely cut off, and who had to satisfy unceasing demands for money and equipments. Large bodies of ragged, barefooted troops continually entered the town, to quit it well shod and with new uniforms. The republican cockade became an abomination in the eyes of the Leghornese, who christened it *il pasticcino*—the little pie—and wrote innumerable lampoons upon its wearers. Leghorn was converted into a camp, and on a large altar in the middle of the *Piazza d'Arme*, a statue of Liberty was erected, at the foot of which the popular representatives, Garat and Salicetti, daily harangued the troops upon parade.—*Vincent Nolte's "Fifty Years in Both Hemispheres."*

The French nobility sank out of sight under the guillotine. The reaction against the Terror had begun before the tricolor had been carried far beyond the boundaries of France; but while the lives of foreigners, not in arms against France, were spared under the milder régime, the substance of the people was consumed in requisitions and exactions for the support of the French troops, and of the cloud of officials who swarmed upon the conquered communities. From these sources were derived the fortunes of French generals and other public men, including Napoleon himself, who seems to have risen from abject poverty to opulence with a speed as astonishing as his military successes.

It may be said that the First Republic never had a fair opportunity to show what it would have done for other countries; but judging from what it did for France, other countries are to be congratulated. It is not probable that Marat and Robespierre and their associates would have been any more merciful to the better classes of Rome, or Vienna, or Berlin, than they were to those of Paris, had the *sans culotte* armies given them the power to play the rôle of Terrorists in those capitals. And while the republican successors of the Terror were more humane, they were likewise more corrupt. They used their victories to levy and extort ransom from States in dread of their arms, and mistook the American people to such a degree as to make a similar attempt on the United States, thus bringing on a naval war between the two nations. It may be repeated, indeed, that the French Republic was simply and solely destructive, the sole and important exception to this characterization being the abolition of the old system of land tenure in France, and the beginning of the creation of a land-owning peasantry, the conservative bulwark of the present Republic.

WHY NAPOLEON FAILED.

Napoleon was not merely a conqueror; he was also one of the greatest of statesmen and lawgivers. He made a sincere attempt to establish liberal institutions in the various countries under his rule, with the reservation that he himself should be the absolute master of all. He had no trouble in obtaining for his usurpation the support of the middle class in France, weary of the narrow oligarchy that tyrannized in the name of liberty, and imitated the corruptions of the Bourbon court, without the prestige of aristocracy. With the Terrorists and Reactionists glaring at each other, Napoleon rode in between and seized the prize of power, risking on the one hand the hate and vengeance of the Jacobins, and on the other the royalist fanaticism of Georges Cadoudal.

It is useless to talk of what Napoleon might have done, had he been let alone. He was not let alone. Even had all the continent been willing to bow to his will, to live at peace with him, and give him opportunity to build up the internal interests of his empire, England would not have permitted him to enjoy rest. The sympathies of the ruling classes in England were aristocratic. The people of England were still controlled by ancient prejudice against their neighbors across the Channel, and in face of the stupendous continental successes of the French, the ministry received almost unanimous support in its policy of war. England maintained the empire of the seas, but Napoleon continued to be supreme on land.

* * * * * *

The wars in which Napoleon was almost continually engaged might well have excused him from the accomplishment of great internal reforms, but he found time, nevertheless, to frame the Code Napoleon, and institute for France and for a great part of Europe, a system of laws which is his lasting monument. He created the code known by his name with the assistance of the ablest lawyers of France, but the work was his own in the sense that it bore his stamp in every section, and carried into effect his carefully matured views of the changes made necessary in the law by the changed conditions of France. The Code Napoleon was to modern times what the Justinian Code had been to the later Roman period. It enfranchised the law from feudalism and ecclesiasticism. It garnered and preserved the best fruit of the Revolution, and provided, at the same time, for that equal and impartial protection of the citizen and his property which is the best guarantee against revolution. So obvious were its benefits, that it has survived all political changes in France, and has continued to be the groundwork of legislation in States unfriendly to France.

It was the expressed desire and purpose of Napoleon to secure in countries under his control the abolition of all pecuniary and other exemptions of the privileged classes, the extinction of all their vested rights to labor, service, tolls and charges on land, and the introduction of a system of equal local rates for all persons. To Jerome, his brother, king of Westphalia, he wrote: "What the German peoples desire with impatience is that individuals who are not noble and who have talents shall have an equal right to your consideration with the nobility; that every sort of servitude and of intermediate obligations between the sovereign and the lowest class in the people should be entirely abolished. The benefits of the Code Napoleon, the publicity of legal procedure, the establishment of the jury system, will be the distinctive characteristics of your monarchy. And to tell you my whole mind on this matter, I count more on the effect of these benefits for the extension and strengthening of your kingdom, than upon the result of the greatest victories. Your people ought to enjoy a liberty, an equality, a well-being unknown to the German peoples. . . . . What people would wish to return to the arbitrary government of Prussia, when it has tasted the benefits of a wise and liberal administration? The peoples of Germany, France, Italy, Spain, desire equality, and demand that liberal ideas should prevail.''

Napoleon found to his cost that the people of Germany and Spain and the Netherlands did wish to return to their old rulers, after they had tasted what he called ''a wise and liberal administration,'' and the reason was that their patriotism was stronger than their gratitude for any benefits that Napoleon could bestow, especially as those benefits were made almost worthless by the exacting demands of a merciless conscription.

The power of Napoleon reached its zenith in the Treaty of Tilsit, and it was under the readjustment of State boundaries and political conditions which followed that the Napoleonic system was most widely developed. The imperial régime, after and in consequence of this treaty, was attended by the reduction of a number of small sovereignties to a subordinate rank, and by the introduction of French laws in the territories annexed to France, or brought under the rule of Napoleon's vassal princes. The emperor sincerely intended, as indicated in his correspondence, that these changes should benefit the people subjected to them. The Germans, however, while more or less sullenly submissive to a master who seemed invincible, continued to regard the French as intruders and oppressors.

* * * * * * *

Two circumstances tended to defeat Napoleon's aim to establish an absolute empire with a foundation of democracy. One of these circumstances was the attempt to buttress his throne with a new nobility, created by himself; the other was the demand for a continuous supply of recruits, made imperative by the exhaustion of his armies in ceaseless warfare. The princes and dukes to whom he awarded titles were.

as a rule, not anxious for the distinctions. Most of them were men of high military rank, who preferred to be known as "Marshal" or "General," rather than as "Prince" this, or "Duke" that, when everybody knew that they were not of princely or ducal ancestry. Napoleon had to order Bernadotte to take the title of Prince of Ponte-Corvo before he would accept it, and others were equally reluctant. The creation of a nobility did not strengthen the empire; but on the contrary it sapped the popular basis of Napoleon's power, without gaining for him the good-will of the dynasties he vainly sought to conciliate by absurd imitation.

The insatiable demand for soldiers to meet the enemies who rose continually on every side of the empire, spurred on by British diplomacy, and subsidized with British gold, was in itself a grievance monstrous enough to more than offset every benefit associated with French supremacy. The departments were swept year after year with the besom of a remorseless conscription, which spared neither the father of a family, nor the widow's son. "In the Prussian States," said a writer of that period, "where the military system is reckoned extremely severe, there are restrictions which humanity claims, which equity prescribes, and which the interests of society demand. The requisition spares, in behalf of the husbandman, the eldest son who is the support of the family; it establishes exceptions in favor of the masters of workshops and manufactories, and admits of exemptions to whole cities and provinces. According to the French law no situation, no condition of life exempts from appearing. The summons to the conscripts of the year 14, which the prefect of the department of the Seine published at the time in Paris, will furnish an idea of it. 'All the conscripts of the year 14,' it is there declared, 'present within the limits of the district, whether married men, widowers or bachelors, susceptible or not susceptible of exemptions, even those who by deformity or disease are evidently incapable of supporting the fatigues of war, are commanded to present themselves in person at the assembly herein pointed out. Persons absent, and those in actual confinement, must be represented by their parents, guardians, friends, or some other person delegated by themselves.' The French law is general and includes no mitigating regulation. The widow's only son; he whose labor is the sole support of a sick or aged father; he who by the death of father or mother has become the parent of a family of helpless brothers and sisters; the young man who has just been, as well as he who is just going to be, married; all are equally seized in its unrelenting grasp. I have seen a conscript, the son of a blind mother, compelled to march. I have seen carried off in three successive years the three sons of a handicraftsman, who had bred them to his own occupation, and who beheld himself, at the age when his strength had left him, bereft of the support to which he had fondly looked during many years of labor and solicitude. . . . . . A mayor who should presume to protect a conscript without being powerfully supported would incur certain ruin. Several mayors have been branded with a hot iron, as guilty of forgery, have been condemned to be exposed to 'the public view' (the pillory), or to the galleys, for having favored certain young men by giving them certificates declaring them incapable of service. Over no operation does terror so arbitrarily preside as over that of the conscription."*

It should be remembered that this military reign of terror extended over provinces of Germany and other countries then subject to France. So great was the dread of punishment for any evasion of the conscription, that when a river in what is now Rhenish Prussia overflowed the ordinary routes of travel, the conscripts plunged

---

* "Sketches of the Internal State of France." M. Faber, 1812.

into the stream up to their necks, and made their way in time to the place appointed for rendezvous. "You are traveling," said the author previously quoted. "Presently you are stopped. A numerous crowd obstructs the highway. The clanking of chains; plaintive voices; an escort of cavalry; naked swords; men pale and emaciated, heads shaven, hideously dressed, dragging fetters and cannon balls, form a shocking procession on the road. Of what atrocious crime, great God! are these miserable wretches guilty, to be reduced to so abject and deplorable a condition? They are refractory conscripts and deserters who, collected in the depots in a department, are transported to a fortress in the interior."

M. Pasquier, who, different from the writer first quoted, was friendly to Napoleon, draws in his Memoirs a deeply impressive picture of the exhaustion of France under militarism. "The number of refractory conscripts," he says, "increased daily to an alarming extent, and it is easy for those who can recall what were then the laws against refractory conscripts, and everything that was devised to punish in the parents the resistance of the children, it is easy, I say, to form an idea of the perturbation which was bound to invade the whole of society from the daily enforcement of laws which had become so odious. The peace of even the most humble dwellings was continually troubled, and the cottage, given up in spite of its poverty to the bailiff, fell a prey to sufferings until then unknown.''

Such is the other side, the sombre side, the human side, of Napoleon's glory and Napoleon's triumphs. France and the adjoining regions were robbed of the flower of their manhood to win the victories and endure the sacrifices which make the story of the First Empire so brilliant and so tragic. "There did not remain," says Pasquier, writing of the levies of 1813, "a single family which was not in terrible anxiety or mourning." What a picture of the Moloch of war! What a price to pay for the fame of having dictated terms to Europe! It is not strange that even in France there were murmurs of rebellion; it would have been strangely unnatural, had German and Hollander and Swiss submitted willingly to the minotaur which devoured them in the name of liberty. It is not strange that the Spaniard concluded that he might better perish fighting for Spain than for France.

* * * * * *

The country which gained most in national spirit, character and development was Italy. "The master carver," says

Professor Thayer, "cut her into several slices to feed his favorite dogs of war; nevertheless she gained much. She woke from torpor to activity; she lived in the Present. Instead of being stranded like a rotting hulk, she was once more swept into the current of European destiny. The Napoleonic administration, though autocratic, was centuries in advance of that of Pope or Bourbon. Antiquated placemen were laid on the shelf. Civilians succeeded to ecclesiastics in every department of government. The Code Napoleon did away with mediæval courts, recognized equality before the law, and promoted respect for justice. Incessant campaigns and the military conscription not only made the Italians fighters—between 1796 and 1814 Italy furnished 360,000 soldiers to the imperial armies—but also broke down provincial barriers and encouraged national spirit. . . . Above all, Italy learned that her petty princes, and even the pope himself, whom Italians had regarded as necessary and incurable evils, could be ousted by a strong hand. Thus were the Italians rejuvenated by contact with the European autocrat; thus did they store up some of the strength and courage which are given out in days of stress and mighty undertakings."*

---
* "Dawn of Italian Independence."

It is significant of the friendly sentiment of Italy toward the Empire that there was no fire in the rear from the Italian people when Napoleon was engaged in the final struggle against his allied enemies. The Italians felt that the Empire had, in their case, constructed, instead of destroying a nation, and they also felt that, however heavy their burdens under Napoleon, those burdens were light compared with the abominable misrule of the petty tyrants whom the French had expelled. The unity and the deliverance of Italy can be directly and clearly traced to the work of the First Napoleon.

Germany, while a grievous sufferer, was also benefited in most important respects by the successes of Napoleon. The old feudal rubbish, which he cast aside as useless, was never again dragged from the attic of the past. Many of the petty sovereigns whom he displaced from their toy principalities were not recalled from obscurity when the tide of war ebbed back beyond the Rhine. The Germans, like the Italians, learned that they were a nation, and the very hatred which they bore the conqueror made their national spirit the stronger. Northern Germany also acquired a prestige and preponderance in German affairs which presaged the consummation of 1870. The Prussians learned the art of war anew from their peerless adversary, and discarding the obsolete system of Frederick the Great, they laid the foundation of that military organization which is now the most perfect in the world.

Russia, whose emperor was arbiter in the readjustment of Europe, after Napoleon, was brought into closer relations than ever before with western powers and became a factor never again to be ignored in the settlement of international issues. England added vastly to her colonial empire, and made up from the plunder of France and Spain and Holland, for her losses in North America. With Napoleon in St. Helena England saw but one rival in the Old World, and that was Russia, and she has been watching Russia ever since.

Spain went back to her Bourbons, and they, with thorough Bourbon bigotry, forthwith resurrected the Inquisition, just as if the car of civilization could be rolled back three centuries by royal decree. Torture was restored, and the common people were sharply taught that they had the same old masters.* Nevertheless, even in Spain the influences springing from French occupa-

---

* The following item of news in a newspaper of 1817—after the Bourbon restoration—reads like a leaf from the fifteenth century. "*Pamplona, Feb. 10th.* On the 2d, 3d and 4th of this month, and in the prison of this city, the torture was inflicted on Captain Olivan, who, for this purpose, was brought down from the citadel, where he had been confined during eight months, merely because he was suspected of

tion and the example of the French Revolution could not be entirely suppressed, and the Bourbon rulers were at length obliged to reluctantly concede some measure of a freeman's rights to their subjects.

* * * * * * *

On the American side of the Atlantic the effects of the French Revolution were hardly less important than in Europe. The revolt of Spanish America, and the separation of Brazil from Portugal, insured an independent future to the American continent. In our own Republic the principles of the French Revolution made a deep impression, and gave an irresistible impulse to democratic ideas. Although the party, now known as Democratic, may perhaps be traced back to the Leisler period in the North and Bacon's Rebellion in the South, the French Revolution infused into that party a spirit which has never been extinguished. It might almost be said that up to a recent period at least, American politics, apart from the slavery struggle, turned on the issues of the French Revolution.

---

disaffection to government. Amidst the most excruciating pangs, no other than energetic declarations of his own innocence were heard, as well as of that of more than thirty other officers confined with him under similar circumstances "

XII.—THE MONROE DECLARATION.

The independence of South America indirectly resulted from Napoleon's conquest of Spain. The Spanish-Americans, like the American colonists before the Revolution, were loyal to the motherland, and when they heard of the French invasion, and the establishment of an alien king in Madrid, they organized, not to assert their own independence, but to aid in driving the stranger from the peninsula. With that fatuous selfishness and intolerance which has always characterized Spanish officialism in the colonies, the viceroys treated the very evidence of the people's loyalty as insubordination, and by their cruelties compelled the colonists to raise in self-defence the standard of revolution.

Arbitrary measures, instead of extinguishing the spirit of independence, only served to enliven its latent sparks and blow them into flame. Miranda died in chains, and Hidalgo, the patriot priest of Mexico, was put to death by his cruel captors, but Bolivar and Paez, Sucre and San Martin, led the patriot armies to ultimate victory, and established the independence of Spanish America. Only one great revolutionary leader, Iturbide, failed to follow the example of Washington. Iturbide attempted to found an imperial dynasty in Mexico, and lost his life and his crown. Bolivar, on the other hand, with a foresight worthy of Washington himself, sought to form a general confederation of all the States of what was formerly Spanish America, with the object of uniting the resources and means of the several States for their general defence and security. This great project was accepted by Chile, Peru and Mexico, and treaties concluded in accordance therewith.

Intelligent self-interest inspired the United States and England to support the independence of South America. England's motive was chiefly commercial and partly political. She wanted Spanish America to be independent because the continent would thus be thrown open to British commerce, and because, not looking forward herself to territorial aggrandizement in that direction, she wished other powers to keep their hands off. The British Government had no desire, in taking this position, to promote the growth and extension of republican institutions. The ruling class in Great Britain would doubtless have preferred to see every Spanish-American State a monarchy, provided that under monarchy it could be equally useful to the British empire and independent of every other European power. If England, in championing the Spanish-

American republics, seemed to champion republican institutions, it was because republican institutions gave the strongest assurance of political separation from Europe, and of a free field for Great Britain.*

On the part of the United States the Monroe Doctrine was the formal and authoritative expression of a sentiment which had animated American breasts from the origin of the Republic. The Monroe Doctrine is based on patriotism and self-preservation, and the crisis which called it forth was of the gravest consequence to the American people. The Spanish empire in America had never been a menace to the United States. It was too decrepit to be dangerous. Conditions would have been very different with France, for instance, or Prussia, established

---

*"The Spanish-American question is essentially settled. There will be no Congress upon it, and things will take their own course on that continent which cannot be otherwise than favorable to us. I have no objection to monarchy in Mexico; quite otherwise. Mr. Harvey's instructions authorize him to countenance and encourage any reasonable project for establishing it (project on the part of the Mexicans I mean), even in the person of a Spanish Infanta. But, as to putting it forward as a project, or proposition of ours, that is out of the question. Monarchy in Mexico, and monarchy in Brazil, would cure the evils of universal democracy, and prevent the drawing of the line of demarkation, which I most dread, America versus Europe. The United States naturally enough aim at this division, and cherish the democracy which leads to it. But I do not much apprehend their influence, even if I believed it. I do not altogether see any of the evidence of their activity in America. Mexico and they are too neighborly to be friends."—*Canning, to the British Minister at Madrid, December 31, 1823.*

as a great South American power. There
was the strongest reason for believing that
the governments of continental Europe
combined in the "Holy Alliance" seriously
intended to dispose the destinies of South
America, as they had divided the continent
of Europe. The primary object of the
allied powers—the proscription of all political reforms originating from the people—
could leave no doubt of the concern and
hostility with which they viewed the development of events in Spanish America,
and the probable establishment of several
independent, free States, resting on institutions emanating from the will and the valor
of the people. But there is more specific
evidence of their hostile intentions—Don
Jose Vaventine Gomez, envoy from the government of Buenos Ayres at Paris, in a
note to the secretary of his government of
the twentieth of April, 1819, said that "the
diminution of republican governments was
a basis of the plans adopted by the Holy
Alliance for the preservation of their thrones
and that in consequence, the republics of
Holland, Venice, and Genoa, received their
deathblow at Vienna, at the very time that
the world was amused by the solemn declaration that all the States of Europe would
be restored to the same situation they were
in before the French Revolution. The
sovereigns assembled at Aix la Chapelle

have agreed, secretly, to draw the Americans to join them in this policy, when Spain should be undeceived, and have renounced the project of re-conquering her provinces; and the king of Portugal warmly promoted this plan through his ministers.'' France also sought by intrigue to secure the acceptance by the United Provinces and Chile of a monarchical government under French protection.

For the reasons before stated these designs naturally alarmed Canning, England's distinguished Minister of Foreign Affairs, and he proposed to Mr. Rush, the American Minister at London, that Great Britain and the United States should join in a protest against European interference with the independent States of Spanish America. This was in September, 1823, and in a message of December 2, following, President Monroe uttered his famous declaration to the effect that ''the United States would consider any attempt on the part of the European powers to extend their system to any portion of this hemisphere as dangerous to our peace and safety.''* Mr. Monroe's motive in issuing this declaration was

---

*"They (the United States) have aided us materially. The Congress (Verona) was broken in all its limbs before, but the President's (Monroe's) speech gives it the coup de grace. While I was hesitating in September what shape to give the protest and declaration I sounded Mr. Rush, the American Minister here, as to his powers and disposition to join in any step which we might take to prevent a

wholly American and patriotic. England's designs were inevitably aided by the action of the American President, and the English Government approved and their press applauded America's resolute course, but it was not to win English applause, but to defend the integrity of the United States that the Monroe Doctrine was proclaimed to the world. The opposition of Great Britain and the attitude of the United States proved more than the Holy Alliance cared to confront, and the nations of Spanish America were allowed to enjoy, without further molestation the independence which they had gained by years of heroic effort and sacrifice.

The "Monroe Doctrine," so-called, has since been accepted by the American people as a principle to be enforced at any cost in their dealings with other nations. The French were compelled to retire from Mexico, the English to take their grasp from Venezuela in obedience to warnings which offered no other choice save war with the United States. Behind those warnings were millions of fighting men of the same

---

hostile enterprise on the part of the European powers against Spanish America. He had not power, but he would have taken upon himself to join with us if we would have begun by recognizing the Spanish-American States This we could not do, and so we went on alone. But I have no doubt that his report to his government of this sounding, which he probably represented as an overture, had a great share in producing the explicit declarations of the President."—*Canning to the British Minister at Madrid.*

race that conquered at Waterloo and Trafalgar, and resources unsurpassed by any nation in the world. Any European power prepared to defy the Monroe Declaration must face America in arms. This is not "jingoism," it is not braggodocio; it is the calm determination of a great people, who have gained their liberties at priceless cost, and who mean that those liberties shall not be imperilled by alien intrusion on the American continent.

The American people make no claim to right of interference with self-rule in the other American republics. Our neighbors can indulge in revolutions and pronunciamentos; they can change their presidents every week and be governed by military dictators, or any other native tyrants as they please—but free from subjection to European power they shall be while an American arm can aim a rifle and an American forge can fashion the armor-plate for our battleships.

President Monroe thought but little, probably, of the full scope of his famous message. It was a declaration of independence for the American continent—the charter of liberty for half the world. European nations have blustered about it, and sneered at it, but they have never yet dared to defy it. When they do, if ever they do, they will find America ready.

XIII.—ENGLAND'S COMMERCIAL TURNING-POINT.

PEEL LAUNCHES FREE TRADE.

The adoption of a free trade policy by Great Britain in 1842, was the commercial turning-point of the century. And yet, while it is true that England has made wonderful progress in commerce and in manufactures since the adoption of a free trade policy, it is equally and historically true that the foundation of England's prosperity was laid, and the strong fabric was erected during a period of protection which lasted for over two centuries, protection which was prohibition in its earlier, and in some forms, of its later stage, and which, not content with a mere embargo on the products of alien nations, inspired the wars, and dictated the policy of the empire in stamping out foreign and colonial rivalry. It was this policy which provoked the American Revolution, and which embroiled England in conflict with the Dutch. The wars against Holland were in the line of commercial aggrandizement, and resulted in the subjection to the English crown and to English commerce of the colonial possessions of that industrious people.

One identical policy guided British administration in dealing with America and with Ireland, and that was to prevent the building up of trade, or the establishment of any industry that might conflict with English monopoly. "The year before the Peace of Ryswick," writes Webber, in his Account of the Woolen Manufactories, quoted in J. Gee's Trade and Navigation (1730), "the English, jealous lest Ireland, by being able to work the woolen goods cheaper than they could do, would by that means supplant them in foreign markets, took the following occasion to cramp their free trade with other nations which they then enjoyed. . . . . It was agreed that Ireland should lay a tax of four shillings on the pound on all woolen goods exported to foreign markets. Upon this England became fearful that the Irish, not having, as before, the opportunity of their foreign trade, might prejudice the English manufactories, by importing woolen goods to England cheaper than we could have them here; and therefore they prohibited the importation of woolen goods from Ireland to England, except only to the five wool ports, and subjected all such goods to duties laid on them by antecedent acts." While America asserted her rights by successful revolution, Ireland, deprived of the manufactures, except flax and linen, which had commenced to flourish, notwithstanding almost continuous and devastating strife, sank into abject industrial as well as political dependence, and into an apathy relieved by occasional spasmodic uprisings against the power which at once enslaved and enfeebled her.

* * * * * *

The policy of protection by heavy import duties afforded to the English producer and manufacturer an ever-extending market, not only in the British Isles, but in the territories which were continually being annexed at the expense of the blood and treasure of the English people, while the wars consequent upon the Revolution in France enabled the British to sweep from the seas the remnant of Continental commerce which had survived previous aggressions. The growth of the British empire, and of British capital and enterprise during the early part of the nineteenth century, proved the effects of protection in building up the wealth and strength of the nation, and had it been only a question of protecting manufacturing industries, England would have had a high tariff to-day. The paramount issue of a free food supply, consequent upon increasing population, overcame, however, all other considerations, and the agriculturists refused to be sacrificed without an accompanying surrender on the part of the manufacturers, among whom, indeed, were found some of the leading advocates of free trade in food.

The movement, which was initiated as an agitation for the repeal of the corn laws, and which had its origin and centre in the manufacturing districts, where the artisans were most severely affected by the prohibitive tariff on corn from abroad, gradually extended in its scope until it embraced a demand for the reduction of duties on all foreign articles to such a scale as might admit of a fair competition with domestic produce, the object being, as stated by Sir Robert Peel in his introductory speech in parliament in 1842, "to make a considerable reduction in the present price of living in England, as compared with the price of living in other countries." Four years later, in the great debate which preceded the adoption of free trade as the commercial policy of England, Sir Robert Peel explained why, in his opinion, England could, under the new policy, continue to command the markets of the world. "We stand," he said, "on the confines of Western Europe, the chief connecting link between the old world and the new. The discoveries of science, the improvements in navigation, have brought us within ten days of St. Petersburg, and will soon bring us within ten days of New York. We have an extent of coast greater, in proportion to our population and the area of our land, than any other great nation, securing to us maritime strength and superiority. Iron and coal, the sinews of manufacture, give us advantages over every rival in the great competition of industry. Our capital far exceeds that which they can command. In ingenuity, in skill, in energy, we are inferior to none."

Such were the cogent reasons advanced by England's leading statesman why the system of protection, pursued for two hundred years, and which had elevated Great Britain to the proud and imperious situation he so eloquently pictured, should give place to free trade. And says Mongredien, himself an earnest supporter of the free trade movement, "the adoption of free trade principles was not the result of pressure from adverse circumstances. The country was flourishing, trade was prosperous, the revenue showed a surplus, railways were being constructed with unexampled rapidity, the working classes were fully and remuneratively employed," and all this under a tariff, which was not only protective, but in some respects prohibitory. The reasons stated by Sir Robert Peel show clearly why England was ready and willing to challenge the competition of the world. She was without a rival; unlimited capital, a degree of skill in manufacture which our American industries are as yet far from having achieved, iron and coal almost at her furnaces, the command of the carrying trade of the world—all these were the weapons and the invincible armor which protection had forged for Great Britain to be armed with in the battle of free trade.

XIV.—LINCOLN'S DEATH-BLOW TO SLAVERY.

The abolition of slavery in the United States was the work of Americans. English agitation of the subject and English abolition in the West Indies had no appreciable effect in promoting the cause of emancipation in America. On the contrary, British attacks on the institution of slavery in the United States had a tendency to arouse resentment on the part of Americans, and to retard and embarrass the steps toward liberation. Nevertheless the anti-slavery agitators in America and England were inspired by a common sentiment—that better sentiment of an age which induced a Howard to devote life and fortune to his suffering fellow men; and which gave birth to a Wilberforce and a Whittier.

The lowest class of labor was the labor of bondmen in nearly all countries until a comparatively recent period. It is an interesting fact that there was a time when the English of both sexes were not only exposed for sale in the markets of Europe, but transported and sold in Africa. Between the fifth and eleventh centuries, indeed, it would have been no abuse of language to call a great part of Englishmen beasts of burden. Our word team, though derived from the original Saxon, which signified children, came nevertheless by its present meaning, from being applied to slaves who ranked with cattle of all kinds, under the general denomination of living money. Dr. Henry tells us in his "History of Great Britain," that, "for some time after the settlement of the Saxons in England, their slaves were in the same circumstances with their horses, oxen, cows and sheep, except that it was not fashionable to kill and eat them."

The Magna Charta secured the rights of freemen only. Servitude of the most abject kind existed long after King John, and was expressly recognized by English law.*

Bondage in England gradually died out, without any special enactment, although it was not until late in the eighteenth century that the last remnant of slavery was abol-

---

* A statute of Edward VI provided that "if any person shall bring to two justices of the peace any runagate servant, or other which liveth idle or loiteringly, by the space of three days, the said justices shall cause the said idle and loitering servant or vagabond, to be marked with a hot iron on the breast, with the mark V, and adjudge him to be a slave of the same person that brought or presented him, to have him, his executors, or assigns, for two years after; so shall he take the said slave, and give him bread, water or small drink, and refuse meat, and cause him to work by beating, chaining, or otherwise. in such work or labour as he shall put him unto, be it never so vile. And if such slave absent himself from the said master within the said term of two years, by the space of fourteen days, then he shall be adjudged by the two justices of the peace, to be marked on the forehead, or the ball of the cheek, with a hot iron, with the sign of an S, and further shall be adjudged to be slave to the said master for ever.

ished in Great Britain by the release of colliers and salters from their obligation to perpetual service. In our own country the form of white servitude known as "redemption"—the sale of labor for a term of years to pay the cost of passage from Europe to America—existed in the early part of the present century.

* * * * * * *

Servitude was abolished in Russia about the beginning of the American Civil War, but it should be unnecessary to say that there was no relation between the emancipation of the Russian serfs and that of the American negroes, although these memorable events occurred within two years of each other. Previous to the Emancipation Act of 1861 all peasants in Russia were serfs of the State, the Crown or the nobility. The soldiers, being at that time, and until 1873, enrolled exclusively from the masses of the peasantry and the burghers, did not return to the condition of serfs on their release from military service, but formed a class by themselves.

The Russian serfs belonging to a private person lived on his land, and cultivated a part of the soil for their own special benefit. This part of the land was called the peasants' lot, and the serfs were bound to till the remainder of the land for their master's benefit. Practically, although not legally, the peasants owned the land they cultivated for their own use. They even enjoyed some vestiges of self-government, and the landlords seldom interfered in their private and personal affairs. The State and Crown peasants were personally free, but under the guardianship of the Department of Crown Lands and of the Ministry of State Domains.

It will be seen, therefore, that there was no similarity between the condition of the American negro slave and that of the Russian serf, although immortal honor attaches to the name of the czar, Alexander II., who, by his ukase of March 3, 1861, emancipated twenty-three millions of his subjects, and by the same memorable decree endowed them not only with freedom, but with communal self-government. It may be that the Russian Emperor had in mind that this great act of justice and of humanity might have a favorable influence on the cause of union and liberty in the United States, but whether such was the case or not, he deserves to be remembered as one of the benefactors of mankind.

* * * * * * *

Negro slavery survived so long, because it was color slavery—the enslavement of a race, which, if not inferior by nature, had become inferior through centuries of barbarism and oppression, to Europeans and their American descendants. The slaveholders saw that only by maintaining this inferiority could slavery be maintained; hence the laws against teaching negroes to read or write. The negro was to be kept as near to the brute as possible, as an excuse for being treated as a brute.

Public sentiment, alike in America and England, was opposed to the slave trade, and it is significant as showing the progress *pari passu* of opinion on both sides of the Atlantic that, while the American Constitution in 1789 provided that the slave trade might be prohibited by Congress not prior to 1808, William Wilberforce, also in 1789, first proposed the abolition of the slave-trade in the House of Commons, and the slave-trade was prohibited by the United States and Great Britain almost simultaneously.

Agitation continued in Great Britain for the abolition of slavery in the British colonies. With England the question was hardly a political one. There were no slaves in Great Britain, and the colonies had no voice in parliament. Jamaica and the other slave-holding islands were helpless, so far as offering any resistance to the will of the British government, and although the West India planters protested earnestly and vigorously, and even uttered empty threats, the Imperial Parliament at length voted to emancipate the slaves, paying to the owners an indemnification amounting to about one hundred millions of dollars.

* * * * * * *

This act of Great Britain, followed by French abolition in 1848, left the United States alone among important and highly civilized nations as a slave-holding country, and here the battle between freedom and slavery was brought to an issue. Here almost from the beginning of the century the nation had been divided in two sections on the slavery question, and it grew in gravity with the progress of the century. The Union, to quote the language of Abraham Lincoln, could not have survived half slave and half free, but slavery might have survived the nineteenth century but for the Fugitive Slave Law and the Kansas-Nebraska bill, which broke down the barriers between the free and slave States, and permitted the slave-owner and slave-hunter to range all over the Union, protected by Federal laws in the possession of human chattels.

In another work* I have endeavored to describe the slavery conflict, and it is unnecessary to repeat that history here. The

---
* "The Land We Live In," Christian Herald Library for 1897.

Fugitive Slave Law was the prologue of the tragedy which ended in the complete emancipation of American slaves. From the day that law was enacted only cowardice on the part of the North could have prevented war, and even then war would only have been postponed, for the South would have demanded more and more guarantees and imposed greater humiliations. Indeed, it brings a blush to the cheeks of a Northern reader even now to see the terms which a Congress controlled by Northern votes was willing to offer to the South to prevent secession, and which the South contemptuously spurned.

The Emancipation Proclamation of President Lincoln, although an act of war, was the long-withheld answer of the North to the Fugitive Slave Law and the repeal of the Missouri Compromise. The victory of Northern arms made the Emancipation Proclamation effective, and slavery ceased in the United States with the surrender of the Confederate armies. The former slaves are now citizens, and, as a rule, law-abiding and industrious citizens.

When slavery fell in the United States it ceased to have standing anywhere. Holland, the only other reputable nation which held slaves up to that time, also conferred freedom in 1863, and Brazil soon after provided for gradual emancipation.

Slavery still exists, but in no part of the world which pretends to be civilized, and the recent extension of European power in Africa has struck a final blow at the very core of the traffic. At last, not in America alone, but wherever Christianity's arm can reach, the cry of Whittier is answered:

"Speak! shall their agony of prayer
  Come thrilling to our hearts in vain?
To us whose fathers scorned to bear
  The paltry menace of a chain;
To us whose boast is loud and long
  Of holy Liberty and Light;
Say shall these writhing slaves of Wrong
  Plead vainly for their plundered Right?"

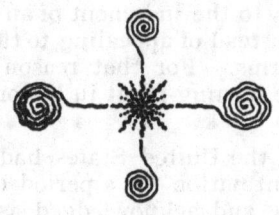

XV.—THE GENEVA TRIBUNAL.

ARBITRATION'S FIRST VICTORY.

Arbitration, as a means of settlement of important international differences, was virtually unknown before the Washington Treaty of 1871. It is true that history is not without instances of the adjustment by a third party of questions at issue between States, or between factions in a State nominally independent of the arbitrator; but it will be found that in every such instance one or both of the parties submitting to arbitration acted in some degree under foreign compulsion. The Geneva Arbitration was the first instance in which two great powers, with an issue at stake which would otherwise have led to war, chose to submit the controversy to the judgment of an impartial tribunal, instead of appealing to the arbitrament of arms. For that reason it was a memorable turning-point in history.

* * * * * * *

In 1860, the United States had been an independent nation for a period of eighty-four years, and acknowledged as such by Great Britain for seventy-seven years. During this period, while sharing to a remarkable extent in the general prosperity of the Christian Powers, they had so conducted their relations toward those Powers as to merit, and they believed that they had secured, the good-will and esteem of all. Their prosperity was the result of honest thrift; their exceptional increase of population was the fruit of a voluntary immigration to their shores; and the vast extension of their domain was acquired by purchase and not by conquest.*

From no people had the United States better right to expect a just judgment than from the people of Great Britain. In 1783, the War of Separation had been closed by a treaty of peace, which adjusted all the questions then pending between the two governments. In 1794, new questions having arisen, growing out of the efforts of France to make the ports of the United States a base of hostile operations against Great Britain, a new treaty was made, at the instance of the United States, by which all the difficulties were arranged satisfactorily to Great Britain, and at the same time so as to preserve the neutrality and the honor of the United States. In the same year, also, the first neutrality act was passed by Congress, prescribing rules and establishing the modes of proceeding to enable the United States to perform their duties as a neutral toward Great Britain and other

---

* See " Papers Relating to the Treaty of Washington—Case of the United States." Government Printing Office, 1872.

belligerents. In 1812, they were forced into war with Great Britain, by the claim of that Power to impress seamen on the high seas from vessels of the United States. After three years the war ceased, and the claim has never since been practically enforced.

In 1818, the United States met British negotiators more than half-way in arranging disputed points about the North American fisheries. In 1827, having added to their own right of discovery the French and Spanish titles to the Pacific coast, they voluntarily agreed to a joint occupation of a disputed portion of this territory, rather than resort to the last arbitrament of nations. In 1838, when a serious rebellion prevailed in Canada, the Congress of the United States, at the request of Great Britain, passed an act authorizing the government to exercise exceptional powers to maintain the national neutrality. In 1842, the Government of the United States met a British envoy in a spirit of conciliation, and adjusted by agreement the disputed boundary between Maine and the British possessions. In 1846, the United States accepted the proposal of Great Britain, made at American suggestion, to adopt the forty-ninth parallel as a compromise line between the two Columbias, and to give to Great Britain the whole of Vancouver's Island.

In 1850, the American Republic waived, by the Clayton-Bulwer Treaty, the right of acquisition on the Isthmus of Panama. In 1854, the American Government conferred upon the people of the British possessions in North America the advantages of a free, full commercial intercourse with the United States for their products, without securing corresponding benefits in return. Thus a series of difficult questions, some of which might have led to war, had been peaceably arranged by negotiations, and the increasing intercourse of the two nations was constantly fostered by continuing acts of friendliness on the part of the government of the United States.

* * * * * * *

All the political relations of the United States with England, with the exception of the episode of the War of 1812, had been those of increasing amity and friendship, confirmed by a repeated yielding of extreme rights, rather than imperil the cordial relations which the United States so much desired to maintain with their nearest neighbors, their best customers, and their blood relations. They had good right, therefore, to believe, and they did believe, that, by virtue of this friendly political understanding, and in consequence of the gradual and steady assimilation of the commercial interests and the financial policies of the two governments, there was in Great Britain, in the summer of 1860, sympathy for the government and affection for the people of the United States. They had equal reason to think that neither the British Government nor people would look with either ignorance or unconcern upon any disaster to them. Above all, they had at that time a right to feel confident that, in any controversy which might grow out of the unhappy existence of African slavery in certain of the Southern States, the British Government would not exercise its sovereign powers, questionably or unquestionably, in favor of the supporters of slavery.

* * * * * * *

Therefore, when the war of secession began, the United States had no cause to anticipate that the course of Great Britain would be, as it proved to be, not only unfriendly, but virtually hostile, to our national government, that the British Government would, as it did, hasten to recognize the Confederacy as a belligerent power even before the British Cabinet had official knowledge that a state of war existed here, and that a Confederate navy would be constructed, armed and manned in British ports to destroy American commerce. Agents of the insurgents acted on British soil as if England was an ally of the Confederacy, and the conduct of the British Cabinet seemed to justify the assumption.

When information against the "Florida" was conveyed to the British Secretary of State for Foreign Affairs, he interposed no objection to her sailing from Liverpool. When the overwhelming proof of the complicity of the Alabama was laid before him, he delayed to act until it was too late, and then, by his neglect to take notice of the notorious criminals, he encouraged the guilty Laird to construct the two rebel rams —the keel of one of them being laid on the same stocks from which the Alabama had just been launched. When the evidence of the character and destination of those rams was brought to his notice, he held it for almost two months, although they were then nearly ready to go to sea, and then at first refused to stop them. Wiser and more just counsels prevailed four days later. But when Mr. Adams, under instructions from his government, transmitted to Earl Russell convincing proof of "a deliberate attempt to establish within the limits of this kingdom (Great Britain) a system of action in direct hostility to the government of the United States," embracing, "not only the building and fitting out of several ships of war under the direction of agents especially commissioned for the purpose, but the preparation of a series of measures under the same auspices for the obtaining from Her Majesty's subjects the pecuniary means essential to the execution of those hostile projects," Lord Russell refused to see in the inclosed papers any evidence of those facts worthy of his attention, or of the action of Her Majesty's government.

Earl Russell spoke against the Union in public speeches, and urged that "the sanguinary conflict" should be brought to an end—of course by the destruction of the Union. He declared in Parliament that the "subjugation of the South by the North" would be "a great calamity," "a calamity to the United States and to the world." Laird, the builder of the Alabama, was cheered when he arose in Parliament to assert that he "would rather be handed down to posterity as the builder of a dozen Alabamas than as the man who applies himself deliberately to get class against class and to cry up the institutions of another country, which, when they came to be tested, are of no value whatever, and which reduced liberty to an utter absurdity."

* * * * * * * * *

Even Mr. Gladstone was carried away by the prejudice of the governing classes of

England against America. "We do not believe," he said, "that the restoration of the American Union by force is attainable. I believe that the public opinion of this country is unanimous upon that subject. (No!) Well, almost unanimous. I may be right or I may be wrong—I do not pretend to interpret exactly the public opinion of the country. I express in regard to it only my private sentiments. But I will go one step further, and say I believe the public opinion of this country bears very strongly on another matter upon which we have heard much, namely, whether the emancipation of the negro race is an object that can be legitimately pursued by means of coercion and bloodshed. I do not believe that a more fatal error was ever committed than when men—of high intelligence, I grant, and of the sincerity of whose philanthropy, I, for one, shall not venture to whisper the smallest doubt—came to the conclusion that the emancipation of the negro race was to be sought, although they could only travel to it by a sea of blood. I do not think there is any real or serious ground for doubt as to the issue of this contest."

As late as the ninth of June, 1864, Earl Russell said in the House of Lords: "It is dreadful to think that hundreds of thousands of men are being slaughtered for the purpose of preventing the Southern States from acting on those very principles of independence which in 1776 were asserted by the whole of America against this country. Only a few years ago the Americans were in the habit, on the Fourth of July, of celebrating the promulgation of the Declaration of Independence, and some eminent friends of mine never failed to make eloquent and stirring orations on those occasions. I wish, while they keep up a useless ceremony—for the present generation of Englishmen are not responsible for the War of Independence—that they had inculcated upon their own minds that they should not go to war with four millions, five millions, or six millions of their fellow-countrymen who want to put the principles of 1776 into operation as regards themselves.''

These sentiments, publicly uttered by members of the British Government, justified the United States in assuming that in permitting armed vessels to go forth from British ports, and fly the flag of the Confederacy as privateers engaged in war against the United States and the destruction of American property, the British authorities were designedly and culpably remiss in the performance of their duties both under international law and the municipal law of Great Britain. The aid given by Great

Britain was an important part of the rebellion. It swept the seas almost clear of the American carrying trade; it supplied the Southern States with many of the necessaries of war, and it helped to prolong the conflict, thereby causing enormous additional expenditure of blood and treasure on the part of the American people. It is not strange that when the Confederacy fell, and the Union was triumphant over its domestic enemies, a general demand arose in the North that Great Britain should be called to account for its share in the conflict. Abraham Lincoln had said, "one war at a time," after the Trent affair, and it seemed that the time had come for another.

* * * * * * *

Fortunately in higher quarters a spirit of conciliation prevailed, and while the government at Washington was determined to obtain redress for the wrongs inflicted, it resolved to exhaust all peaceable and honorable means before resorting to the decision of arms. After prolonged negotiations the Treaty of Washingto , signed in May, and ratified in June, 1871, provided that all complaints and claims growing out of the escape of the "Alabama" and other Anglo-Confederate war vessels from British ports should be "referred to a Tribunal of Arbitration, to be composed of five arbitrators,

to be appointed in the following manner, that is to say: One shall be named by the President of the United States; one shall be named by Her Britannic Majesty; His Majesty the King of Italy shall be requested to name one; the President of the Swiss Confederation shall be requested to name one, and His Majesty the Emperor of Brazil shall be requested to name one."
"In case of the death, absence, or incapacity to serve of any or either of the said arbitrators, or in the event of either of the said arbitrators omitting or declining or ceasing to act as such, the President of the United States, or Her Britannic Majesty, or His Majesty the King of Italy, or the President of the Swiss Confederation, or His Majesty the Emperor of Brazil, as the case may be, may forthwith name another person to act as arbitrator in the place and stead of the arbitrator originally named by such head of a State. And in the event of the refusal or omission for two months after receipt of the request from either of the contracting parties of His Majesty the King of Italy, or the President of the Swiss Confederation, or His Majesty the Emperor of Brazil, to name an arbitrator, either to fill the original appointment, or in the place of one who may have died, be absent, or incapacitated, or who may omit, decline, or from any cause cease to act as

such arbitrator, His Majesty the King of Sweden and Norway shall be requested to name one or more persons, as the case may be, to act as such arbitrator or arbitrators.''

The Tribunal of Arbitration was to meet at Geneva, Switzerland, and the decision of the Tribunal to be delivered, if possible, within three months after the close of the arguments on both sides. The contracting parties engaged to consider the result of the proceedings as a full, perfect and final settlement. The Tribunal awarded $15,500,000 damages in gold for the vessels and cargoes destroyed by the three Anglo-Confederate cruisers and their tenders, and this amount was paid over to the United States by Great Britain.

* * * * * * *

The principle of arbitration has been applied to other issues between the United States and Great Britain, the most signal instance being that of the disputed Venezuela boundary, in which the United States appeared as the champion of the weak South American State, and compelled England to withdraw from the arrogant position which that country has commonly assumed toward inferior nations. It is to be noted, however, that the principle of international arbitration has not yet been generally accepted, and that in the cases where it has prevailed the parties interested adopted it, not from motives of humanity, but wholly from self-interest. England was defeated in the fall of the Confederacy, and accepted arbitration as a dignified cover for retreat from an untenable position. The British had no desire to do directly the fighting which they had helped others to do. They had failed in attempting to break down the Union with batteries masked by Confederate redoubts, and they wanted to resume friendly relations with the power they could not destroy. The American people, on the other hand, were in a temper to fight both France and England, if necessary, in vindication of American rights, and to punish indirect attacks on the security and unity of the Republic. Both France and England counted the cost, and both yielded to American demands, France by withdrawing from Mexico, and England by consenting to the arbitration of an issue which no honorable arbitrator could decide in her favor.

Arbitration has, therefore, so far been accepted not as a substitute for war, but as a plan to be resorted to when less expensive than war and more honorable than surrender. It is significant that great powers in dealing with lesser States refuse to countenance arbitration. When they know the advantage of strength to be on their side they stand upon that advantage, and they accept arbitration only when war would be certain to cost them more than a peaceable adjustment. In other words, arbitration so far has been a recognition, not of justice, but of force. This is not a satisfactory or a promising condition of affairs. International arbitration should be founded, like judicial decisions between man and man, on a general recognition of what is right and what is wrong, and a general determination that the right shall prevail. Until that time comes civilized nations will not be far in advance of the barbarous tribes of the forest in the settlement of their mutual difficulties, save in the refinement and ingenuity of mutual slaughter. Nevertheless the Alabama Claims arbitration was a grand step toward universal peace and goodwill, and the United States, as the party that had been signally injured and whose patience and magnanimity made arbitration possible, can point with satisfaction, that will grow as years roll on, to the Treaty of Washington.

XVI.—INDUSTRIAL TURNING POINTS.

WATT MAKES STEAM WORK.

Greater in its influence on mankind than any invention since printing, the discovery of steam power was the most important event of the eighteenth century. Europeans had visited America before Columbus, and Watt was not the first to perceive and study the qualities of steam. The ancients knew something of its force, and as early as 1623, Solomon de Caus, a French engineer, published a book in Paris on "moving forces," in which he said that "if water be sufficiently heated in a close ball of copper, the air or steam arising from it will at last burst the ball with a noise like the going off of a petard." He also actually describes a method of raising water, as he expresses it, by the aid of fire, which consists in the insertion in the containing vessel of a perpendicular tube reaching nearly to its bottom, through which, he says, all the water will rise when sufficiently heated. The agent here is the steam produced from part of the water by the heat, which, acting by its expansive force upon the rest of the water, forces it to make its escape in a jet through the tube, the supply of the water being kept up through a cock in the side of the vessel. Later in the seventeenth century the Marquis of Worcester described in his wonderful discoveries of the age what he called "an admirable and most forcible way to drive up water by fire." "I have seen," he says, "the water run like a constant fountain-stream forty feet high; one vessel of water rarefied by fire driveth up forty of cold water." Sir Samuel Morland, Denis Papin, Savery and other ingenious persons gave the world from time to time new information about the effects of heated water and steam. The invention, however, most worthy of notice previous to Watt was an engine constructed about the year 1711 by Thomas Newcomen, an ironmonger, and John Calley, a glazier, both of Dartmouth, in Devonshire, England. This contrivance proceeded on the principle of making steam the moving power in the machinery, the weight of the atmosphere acting upon a piston so as to carry it down through a vacuum created by the condensation of the steam. Newcomen's engine was applied to various important purposes, but it was by no means capable of securing the complete command of the energies of steam. It is most noteworthy as having been the immediate object-lesson which suggested Watt's great invention.

* * * * * * *

James Watt, a native of Greenock, Scotland, was from boyhood deeply interested in mechanical science. He was mathematical instrument maker to the college at Glasgow, and his association with Dr. Black and other distinguished members of the University served greatly to enlarge his knowledge and sharpen his instinct for scientific research. After living some years at the college Watt removed to the city, and entered upon the profession of a general engineer. He acquired a high reputation and was extensively employed in making surveys and estimates for canals, harbors, bridges and other public works.

While attending to his duties as engineer he found time to study the employment of steam as a mechanical agent, a subject to which his attention had been directed by Dr. John Robison, of Glasgow University, an author of treatises on mechanics.

A model of Newcomen's engine having been sent to Watt in the winter of 1763-4 he perceived its imperfections and began to turn in his mind the possibility of employing steam in some new manner which should enable it to operate with much more powerful effect. Having become possessed of this idea, Watt started on a series of experiments for the purpose of ascertaining as many facts as possible with regard to the properties of steam. He found that the rapidity with which the water evaporated depended simply on the quantity of heat which was made to enter it, and this again on the extent of the surface exposed to the fire. He also ascertained the quantity of coal necessary for the evaporation of any given quantity of water, the heat at which the water boiled under various pressures, and many other particulars never before accurately determined.

It is needless to follow Watt through the series of experiments and discoveries which resulted in the construction of a real steam engine, and which entitle him to be regarded as the author of the practical use of steam as the chief motive power in our modern civilization. Without pecuniary resources of his own, and without friends willing to risk their money in his behalf, he struggled along under much discouragement. At length he found a helper in Dr. Roebuck, of the Carron ironworks, near Glasgow, and an engine was constructed with a cylinder of eighteen inches diameter, which, although far from perfect in all its parts, demonstrated the great value of Watt's improvements. Owing to pecuniary difficulties Dr. Roebuck had to withdraw from the enterpirse, and Watt formed a connection with Boulton. the eminent hardware manufacturer of Birmingham. The firm of Boulton and Watt commenced the business of engine-making in 1775, and from that year may be dated the age of steam.

* * * * * * *

MURDOCK GIVES LIGHT.

It is an interesting fact that the manufactory of Messrs. Boulton and Watt was one of the first places lighted with gas distilled from coal. To William Murdock belongs the credit, not of discovering the illuminating power of gas, but of putting it to practical use, and the inventor of the steam engine was among the earliest to perceive the value of Murdock's experiment. Gas has been a most important factor in building up nineteenth century civilization, especially in our large cities. It is a potent moral agent, a foe of public disorder and revolution, and it would have been difficult, if not impossible, for science and industry to have achieved their present conditions without illuminating gas.

* * * * * * *

FULTON PLOUGHS THE HUDSON.

To an American, Robert Fulton, is due the application of steam-power to the movement of vessels in the water. Fulton was born in Lancaster County, Pennsylvania, in the year 1765; his father died in 1768, leaving little patrimony to his children. Robert Fulton, the son, was attached in his youth to drawing and painting, and from his earnings and savings in this profession between his seventeenth and twenty-second year, he purchased a small farm in Washington County, Pennsylvania, on which he settled his mother; who remained on it till her death in 1799. Fulton, therefore, commenced his career of life by sacrificing the profits of his earliest exertions to make his surviving parent comfortable and independent. This was a commencement of excellent augury.

Fulton went to England to study painting. While in that country he turned his attention to the construction and use of navigable canals, a subject then of the greatest interest both in America and Europe. He invented a torpedo for the destruction of vessels of war, and at length he approached the great problem, the solution of which was to earn for him the gratitude of mankind—steam navigation.

Others had attempted to navigate vessels by means of steam, but until Fulton undertook the task, no one had succeeded in the attempt for any practical or useful purpose. Fulton was fortunate in encountering at an early date in his efforts the Hon. Robert

R. Livingston, American Minister to France, who was himself interested in steam navigation. Mr. Livingston had, in March, 1798, obtained an exclusive right for steam navigation from the New York Legislature, but his experiments were abortive as to any practical utility. He had the merit, however, of rightly appreciating Mr. Fulton's talents. He joined Mr. Fulton in the plan of steam navigation; and in 1803 they jointly built a boat which was propelled by steam on the Seine, at Paris, with so much success, that, on their return to New York, in 1806, the project was put in execution without delay. Fulton gave directions for a steam engine to Boulton and Watt, which was executed in such a manner as to give the experiment fair play. With this engine the first successful steamboat, built under Fulton's direction, navigated the Hudson in 1807.

To show how little pretensions the English have to this discovery, I quote the following extract from the London Monthly Magazine for October, 1813: "We have made it our special business to lay before the public all the particulars we have been able to collect relative to the invention of steam passage boats in America, and their introduction into Great Britain; because we consider this invention as worth to mankind more than a hundred battles gained, or towns taken, even if the victors were engaged in a war, which might have some pretence to be called defensive and necessary."

The history of the steamboat, since Fulton, would be a history of navigation, indeed, of civilization. The steamboat has brought Europe and America within a few days' distance of each other. It has enabled commerce to penetrate every sea; it bears the missionary and the trader into the heart of Africa, and propels the vast machines of traffic, of pleasure and of war, compared with which the vessels of the Armada, of Drake and Magellan were pigmies.

* * * * * * *

STEPHENSON'S "ROCKET" FLIES.

It is a singular fact that although railways had been in use in the transfer of coal from mines to places of shipment in the early part of the seventeenth century, it was not until 1830, many years after the success of steam navigation had been demonstrated, that the first steam railway was opened for traffic.

Considerable credit is due to Richard Trevithick for his invention of a self-acting steam carriage, for which he took out a patent in 1802, and which successfully drew railway wagons at Merthyr-Tydvil in 1804.

This, the first locomotive, drew only ten tons of bar iron at the rate of five miles an hour. It appears to have been Trevithick's intention to move carriages for the ordinary use of traffic by means of his locomotive, but the public did not view his plan with favor, and the powerful canal interests, in which large capital was invested, discouraged any improvement in the direction of land carriage.

* * * * * * *

George Stephenson made railway travel by steam-power practical, and was the founder of the railway systems of to-day. The career of Stephenson had its lesson of deepest interest and value for every man laboring against apparently insurmountable difficulties. His father supported a family of six by tending a colliery engine for twelve shillings—about three dollars—a week. Young Stephenson was glad to eke out the family income by herding cows for four cents a day, and later on hoeing turnips at eight cents a day. Being appointed fireman in a colliery, he gave himself to the study of the steam engine. It is of interest to note that when but twenty-one years of age he married a young woman of his own station in life, but was left a widower two years later.

Stephenson managed to pay eight cents

a week out of his earnings for lessons in reading, writing and arithmetic. He had a hard struggle, and wept bitterly, he tells us, over the thought that he might have to emigrate. He first attracted public attention by inventing a colliery safety-lamp, which brought him some income. He was then about thirty-five years of age, and three years later he married his second wife, the daughter of a farmer. About the same time he constructed his first locomotive, and his great improvement, the "steam-blast," made rapid railway travel possible. In 1821, Stephenson was appointed engineer for the construction of the Stockton and Darlington Railway, which, however, could not be considered a railway in the modern sense, and soon afterward he was chosen engineer of the proposed line between Liverpool and Manchester.

When Stephenson's locomotive, the "Rocket," proved itself capable of going at the speed of twenty-five miles an hour the world awoke at last to the possibilities of steam travel. Said a writer of 1831: "Another application of steam which has been made only within the last few months is perhaps destined to be productive of still greater changes in the condition of society than have resulted from any of its previous achievements. It had been employed several years ago at some of our collieries in the propelling of heavily loaded carriages over railways; but the great experiment of the Liverpool and Manchester Railway has, for the first time, demonstrated with what hitherto almost undreamt-of rapidity traveling by land may hereafter be carried on through the aid of steam. Coaches, under the impetus communicated by this, the most potent and at the same time the most perfectly controllable of all our mechanical agencies, have already been drawn forward at the flying speed of thirty and thirty-two miles an hour. If so much has been done already it would be rash to conclude that even this is to be our ultimate limit of attainment. . . . . But even when the rate of land traveling already shown to be quite practicable shall have become universal, in what a new state of society shall we find ourselves! When we shall be able to travel a hundred miles in any direction in six or eight hours, into what comparative neighborhood will the remotest extremes, even of a large country, be brought, and how little shall we think of what we now call distance! A nation will then indeed be a community; and all the benefits of the highest civilization, instead of being confined to one central spot, will be diffused equally over the land, like the light of heaven. This improvement, in short, when fully consummated, will confer upon man nearly as much new power and new enjoyment as if he were actually endowed with wings."

Steam has already far surpassed even the prediction which we have quoted. It is the right arm of civilization, laboring unceasingly in the field, the factory, the mart of trade and the dwelling-place of civilized man. It has made possible the industrial system of to-day, with its gigantic concentration of human and mechanical energies; a system which seems to render inevitable, within the coming century, social and political changes of the most radical character.

* * * * * * *

FRANKLIN DRAWS THE LIGHTNING.

Some one has said that "Franklin drew the lightning from the sky and Morse made it speak." While ancients as well as moderns had some knowledge of electricity, it was not until the year 1746 that the discovery was made of the possibility of accumulating large quanties of the electric fluid by means of what was called the Leyden jar, or phial. The announcement of the wonders of the Leyden jar excited the curiosity of all Europe, and led to many experiments by persons interested in the new and mysterious power. Dr. Franklin witnessed some of these experiments at Boston, and when he went back to Philadelphia, soon after, he devoted much of his time to electrical study. He did not rest content with ascertaining the principle of the Leyden phial, but made an application of the principle in the construction of an electrical battery. He also proved that lightning was caused by electricity. "If two gun-barrels electrified," he said, "will strike at two inches distance and make a loud report, at how great a distance will ten thousand acres of electrified cloud strike, and give its fire; and how loud must be that crack!" Franklin's experiment with the kite and key has often been related. Seeing a thunderstorm approaching he took a walk into a field in which there was a shed. He was accompanied by his son to assist him in his experiments. They carried with them a kite, made of a large silk handkerchief, stretched over two crosssticks, this simple apparatus being intended to draw the lightning from its cloud. The kite was held by a hempen string. The kite being raised, Franklin fastened a key to the lower extremity of the string, and then insulating it by attaching it to a post by means of silk, he placed himself under the shed, and awaited the result.

For some time no signs of electricity appeared. A cloud, apparently charged with lightning, had even passed over them without producing any effect. At length, however, just as Franklin was beginning to despair, he observed some loose threads of the hempen string rise and stand erect, exactly as if they had been repelled from each other by being charged with electricity. He immediately presented his knuckle to the key, and to his inexpressible delight, drew from it the electrified spark. It is said that his emotion was so great at this completion of a discovery which was to make his name immortal that he heaved a deep sigh, and felt at that moment he would have willingly died. As the rain increased the cord became a better conductor and the key gave out electricity copiously.

Franklin also ascertained by experiment that distance made virtually no difference of time in the passage of electricity. In a circuit of several miles he could observe no difference of time between the touch at one extreme and the spark at the other. We have the authority of Professor Samuel Finley Breese Morse himself that it was Franklin's experiments which suggested to Morse the transmission of intelligence by means of the electric wire.

* * * * * * *

MORSE'S HAPPY THOUGHT ON SHIPBOARD.

Professor Morse was, as he himself states, not deep in the mysteries of electricity.

Having come to the conclusion that the electric current could be transmitted instantaneously, he applied himself to the discovery of some practical method for conveying intelligence by means of that current; and doubtless this concentration of his energies on the one practical point, irrespective of abstract research and experiment, had much to do with his success in a field neglected by men much deeper in electrical science. Professor Morse says, in defending his claim to the invention of telegraphy:

"From the autumn of the year 1829 till the autumn of the year 1832, I was in Europe, principally in Italy. I conceived the telegraph on board the ship (Sully), in 1832, while on my return home, essentially as it now exists. It was operated in my rooms before numerous persons, my pupils and others, in 1835; it was exhibited to a large audience of a thousand or more persons through ten miles of wire in the New York City University in the autumn of 1837; to a committee of the Franklin Institute in Philadelphia in January, 1838; to Congress and the Cabinet at Washington for three months in the early part of that year; to the Academy of Sciences and thousands of visitors in Paris in the autumn of 1838; to members of the Royal Society of both Houses of Parliament, and the Lords of the Admiralty at Lord Lincoln's in London, in the month of March, 1839, and after all this I first became acquainted, either personally or by correspondence, with Professor Henry.''

The Professor Henry alluded to was Professor Joseph Henry, of Princeton College, to whom Professor Morse applied for some information on the subject of electricity, after the Morse invention had been completed, and who was mentioned by some people as the real author of telegraphy. On this question the following written by Professor Henry to Professor Morse in 1842, ought to be decisive:

"The idea of transmitting intelligence to a distance by means of electric action has been suggested by various persons from the time of Franklin to the present; but until within the last few years, or since the principal discoveries in electro-magnetism, all attempts to reduce it to practice were necessarily unsuccessful. The mere suggestion, however, of a scheme of this kind is a matter for which little credit can be claimed, since it is one which would naturally arise in the mind of almost any person familiar with the phenomena of electricity; but the bringing it forward at the proper moment, when the developments of science are able to furnish the means of certain success, and the devising of a plan for carrying it into practical operation, are the grounds of a first claim to scientific reputation, as well as public patronage."

Professor Morse was always indignant at any intimation that his invention did not originate with himself, and on this point he makes the following sound observations regarding inventions in general:

"It is often assumed that an invention is prompted and perfected by a knowledge of former attempts by others to realize a similar result. The dates of these are recorded in chronological sequence, as if the latter attempts depended upon and were the resultants of the former. Such sequence is often imaginary. Indeed, it seldom exists. It is much more frequently the case that an invention is conceived and perfected wholly in ignorance of any previous attempts by others."

* * * * * * *

"It was at table in the cabin," wrote Professor Morse to Dr. Charles T. Jackson, of Boston, another claimant, "just after we had completed the usual repast at midday. We were conversing on recent scientific discoveries. The question was asked by a passenger if electricity was retarded by the length of the wire. You replied no, that the electricity passed instantaneously over any known length of wire, and you then alluded, in proof, to the experiment of Dr. Franklin, who had made many miles in circuit near Philadelphia (London). He ascertained the velocity of electricity, but could observe no difference of time between the touch at one extreme and the spark at the other. I then remarked, 'This being so, if the presence of electricity can be made visible in any desired part of the circuit I see no reason why intelligence should not be transmitted instantaneously by electricity.'"

Professor Morse then relates how he lay awake at night thinking over the problem, and how he devised a system of signs, and constructed a species of type, which he drew in his sketch-book, and by which he proposed to regulate the passage of electricity.

The struggle was not over when Professor Morse had worked out his plan of telegraphy. He filed his caveat at Washington in 1837, and made a public exhibition of his discovery in the same year. During several years following he appealed in vain to Congress and to foreign governments for aid in establishing a telegraph line. At length, when Morse had almost given up hope, Congress, in the last moments of the session of 1843, appropriated $30,000 for an experimental line between Washington and Baltimore. After the success of his system had been fully demonstrated, Professor Morse had to face long and expensive litigations in defence of his rights; but he finally triumphed over every obstacle, and in the latter part of his life he enjoyed in full measure the honor and wealth which he had so arduously earned.

* * * * * * *

CYRUS FIELD'S FIRST CABLE MESSAGE—
"GLORY TO GOD IN THE HIGHEST."

Professor Morse was the author of the idea of submarine telegraphy. About the same time that he originated his land telegraph system he announced to the Secretary of the Treasury "that a telegraphic communication on his plan might, with certainty, be established across the Atlantic." To the late Cyrus W. Field, however, is due the credit for having carried the idea into practice, after surmounting with patience, energy and enterprise unsurpassed difficulties and disappointments which would have amply excused failure. "Europe and America are united by telegraph. Glory to God in the highest; on earth peace and good will towards men," were the words that flashed under the ocean, August 17, 1858. This cable ceased working after a few weeks, and the great civil war soon afterward distracted the American people from everything save that tremendous conflict. Disaster again attended the plan to lay a cable in 1865, but in 1866 the undertaking was renewed, and successfully accomplished, and from that time to the present communication by submarine telegraph between America and Europe has been an established fact. So perfect and convenient is that communication that, when a great storm interrupted telegraphic communication between New York and Boston—a distance of about two hundred and forty miles—in March, 1888, messages were exchanged between the two cities under the ocean by way of London.

* * * * * * *

The value of telegraphy to mankind is inestimable. In addition to its uses in commerce and trade, and the personal affairs of life, it makes the whole civilized world a board of censors on the actions of public men everywhere. Through the telegraph public opinion in all parts of the globe is brought to bear simultaneously on the course of events. Wars are often thus prevented, and peace, when it comes, puts an immediate end to conflict. The War of 1812, for instance, lasted for months, and its principal battle was fought after peace had been declared. Thousands of lives would have been saved if the Treaty of

Ghent could have been made known at once in New Orleans.

The cable bearing to every part of civilization news of the brave battle of the Boers in defence of their liberties quickened public sentiment in their behalf, and was instrumental in staying the arm of England, outstretched to destroy them. Had the fight at Majuba Mountain occurred before the age of the telegraph, England would have avenged the defeat and crushed the Boers before the rest of mankind had even learned that the struggle was going on. Barbarism, as well as civilization, feels the influence of the electric spark flashing its light into those dark places of the earth, which, the inspired writings say, are "the habitations of cruelty." The Sultan in his chamber, the autocrat in his fortress-palace, are compelled to bow to the power which the telegraph evokes.

* * * * * * *

BELL AND EDISON MAKE LIGHTNING TALK.

The telephone, invented about twenty years ago by Alexander Graham Bell, and made practical by Thomas A. Edison and others, seems to promise a time when men will converse with each other, though thousands of miles apart. It is generally believed that the telephone, already in general use, would have been made far more useful than it is now, but for the restricting influence upon its development of the vast capital invested in telegraph systems.

The electric light, in the improvement of which Edison has added greatly to his fame, besides acquiring large wealth, is turning night into day in many of our cities, and is coming into use also in factories, shops and dwellings, instead of gaslight, although gas continues to be profitable to its makers and acceptable to the public.

* * * * * * *

STEAM'S FELLOW-TITAN.

The greatest recent development in electrical science has been the conversion of electricity into mechanical power. Electricity, as a motive power, is where steam was when Fulton launched his first steamboat. Its possibilities seem incalculable. It can be conducted great distances from the source of supply, and bring Niagara to the doors of New York. It can utilize the far-away mountain stream in running the machinery of the city factory. It may yet, in a vast degree, supersede steam, and it may be that in the harnessing of our great American cataract we witness another turning-point of the centuries.

* * * * * * *

ARKWRIGHT'S SPINNING MACHINE—HOW A BARBER BECAME A NOBLEMAN.

It is not the purpose of the compiler of this work to indulge in observations on the political economy of machinery or to discuss the arguments advanced for and agaiust the industrial conditions that have arisen within the present century. This book is intended to deal with facts, not with theories. It may be proper, however, to remark that there is much to be said on both sides of the machinery and labor-saving question, and that a great good may become an evil when carried to extremes. The changes which have occurred since machines run by water and steam-power took the place of handiwork have added to national wealth at some cost of individual independence, and have made the luxuries of the past the cheap and general comforts of the present. To a certain limit they broadened the field of labor, but the evidence is now altogether too manifest that the limit has been passed, and that the tendency of concentrated capital, with machinery as its weapon, is to restrict the opportunity of the toiler to earn a living for himself and his family.

Until the middle of the eighteenth century manufacturing was almost universally

—as the word itself indicates—handiwork, aided by rude implements, and a few recent improvements, which still left the operative in a large degree his own master. There were master manufacturers, but they depended upon the cottagers for their material, and the latter were in a position more like that of contractors than of employes bound to certain hours of service.

* * * * * * *

The manufacture of cotton goods in England received a considerable impetus, about 1760, from increased exportation to America and to the continent. The thread had hitherto been spun entirely by the tedious process of the distaff and spindle, the spinner drawing out only a single thread at a time. As the demand for the manufactured article continued to increase, a greater and greater scarcity of weft was experienced, till, at last, although there were fifty thousand spindles constantly at work in Lancashire alone, each occupying an individual spinner, they were insufficient to supply the quantity of thread required. The weavers generally in those days had the weft used spun for them by the females of their family. Those weavers whose families could not furnish the necessary supply of weft had their spinning done by their neighbors, and were obliged to pay more for the spinning than the price allowed by their masters.

It was no uncommon thing for a weaver to walk three or four miles in a morning, and call on five or six spinners, before he could collect weft to serve him for the remainder of the day, and when he wished to weave a piece in a shorter time than usual, a new ribbon or gown was necessary to quicken the exertions of the spinner.*

It was natural, under these circumstances, that ingenious individuals should turn their attention to contrive some improved method of spinning, and it was then that a man working at the humble calling of a barber conceived and invented the machinery which eventually superseded the cottage system of manufacturing.

* * * * * * *

Sir Richard Arkwright was born at Preston, in Lancashire, England, in 1732, of very poor parents, being the youngest of thirteen children. He had very little, if any, schooling, and was brought up to the barber's trade, which he followed until thirty years of age. Arkwright had a genius for mechanics, which even his monotonous routine at the barber's chair could not suppress. He became acquainted with a clockmaker named Kay, and from this

---
*Guest's "History of the Cotton Manufacture."

connection dates his entrance upon a new career.

Arkwright and Kay appeared at Preston in 1767, and occupied themselves with the erection of a machine for spinning cotton thread, of which they brought a model with them. They prevailed upon a Mr. Smalley, who is described as a liquor merchant and painter, to join them in their speculation, and the machine was put together in the parlor of the dwelling-house attached to the free grammar school, the use of which Smalley had obtained from his friend, the schoolmaster. At that time Arkwright was so poor that, an election taking place in the town, his friends had to subscribe to get him a new suit of clothes before he could present himself at the poll-room.

As soon as the election was over Arkwright and Kay moved to Nottingham, being apprehensive of the hostility of the people of Lancashire to the introduction of spinning by machinery. There Arkwright submitted his model to Messrs. Need and Strutt, stocking makers of that place. Mr. Strutt, who was himself an ingenious student of mechanics, inspected the model and saw its value, and he and Mr. Need at once agreed to enter into partnership with Arkwright, who accordingly, in 1769, took out a patent for the machine as its inventor. A spinning mill, drawn by horse-power, was at the same time erected and filled with the frames.

Arkwright did not claim to be in all respects the inventor of the machinery known by his name. He admitted that as to some of the designs included in his patent he had improved rather than invented. He attributed the conception of the spinning-jenny to one Hargreaves, who had lived at Blackburn, and who had been driven out of Lancashire in consequence of his invention, and died in obscurity and distress.

Arkwright's invention was the turning-point in giving to England pre-eminence in manufactures, and was the starting-point of cotton manufactures in America. Arkwright was fought on every side by the very manufacturers whom he did so much to benefit, and his principal patent was annulled by the adverse decision of a jury. His remarkable energy, however, carried him through every struggle, and his business ability enabled him to accumulate a considerable fortune. A few years before his death he received the honor of knighthood.

* * * * * * *

HOW SLATER SMUGGLED ARKWRIGHT'S MACHINE IN HIS BRAIN.

Samuel Slater, the father of cotton manufactures in America, was an apprentice to

Strutt, the partner of Arkwright. The laws of England forbade anyone to convey models out of the country, and Slater, when he determined to emigrate to the United States, had to rely upon his memory for the reproduction of the Arkwright machinery. Slater was fortunate in attracting the attention of Moses Brown, an eminent merchant, of Providence, R. I., with whose aid he established his first factory at Pawtucket, in that State.

* * * * * * *

Aided by water-power, steam and gas, and with electric power also recently brought into service, manufacturing has grown enormously in every civilized country, and especially in the United States and Western Europe. In the United States, in England, in Germany, Belgium and France, the markets are generally over-supplied with goods, as compared with the ability of the people to buy, and protective barriers have been raised nearly everywhere, save in Great Britain and Belgium, to preserve the native market to the resident manufacturers. And while the markets are thus glutted with an over-abundance of manufactured goods, and multitudes are clamoring in vain for leave to toil, inventive genius is at work in both hemispheres seeking to make it possible for the employer to get along with fewer employes by means of labor-saving machines.

Thus the ranks of unemployed labor are continually recruited through labor-saving inventions, and in this country, also, through virtually unrestricted immigration. The barrier of protection is raised higher and higher on this side of the Atlantic only to be challenged by ingenious devices for reducing the cost of production on the other side. Tidings of prosperity in English or German manufacturing centres are received with a pang, as if it were a blow at ourselves, while the news that operatives in this or that part of Europe have been driven to the soup-house and suicide is hailed with hardly concealed satisfaction.

* * * * * * *

The market for labor is being still further narrowed by the formation of vast combinations of capital, generally known as "trusts," which control certain lines of production. The "trusts," with the reasonable purpose of making all the profit they can, keep down expenses to the lowest limit consistent with efficient management, and close factories wherever factories are deemed unnecessary. They are able to apply all the power and energy of concentrated capital, directed by individual ability, and the best services that wealth can command.

Legislation has been enacted to suppress "trusts," but such legislation being repugnant to free institutions and to individual rights, is of no effect in practice.

It is obviously as fair, from a moral and common-sense standpoint, for an individual to put his capital into a "trust" as to put it into any other form of investment, and to deny him that right is to abridge his freedom as a citizen. The "trust" may be dangerous, but it is logical. It is the commercial energy of the age carried to an extreme.

The "trusts," however, are blazing the way to State socialism. The people are instinctively opposed to the "trust" system, and it seems plain enough that the people will eventually conclude that if all the business of the country in certain important lines is to be concentrated in a few hands, if individualism and competition are to disappear, the people might as well form a "trust" of their own, and apply to the general uses the profits which now go to swell enormous fortunes. I am not suggesting this result as one to be approved. I am an advocate of individualism, and have always been opposed to socialism, but now that individualism is disappearing under the pressure of concentrated capital, and of the Titanic tools which invention has placed at the command of capital, it seems to me inevitable that the people will ultimately prefer State socialism to an oligarchy of "trusts," competition, the most powerful bulwark against State socialism, having been effaced by the "trusts" themselves.

The cry for municipal ownership is simply the beginning of State socialism. It is already a strong movement, and gaining in strength, and the indications are that the twentieth century will dawn upon the American people entering upon this new struggle —this probably final phase of the industrial revolution.

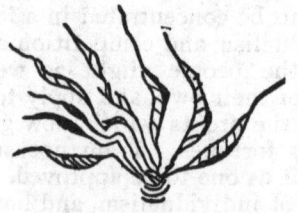

XVII.—TEN MILITARY AND NAVAL TURNING POINTS.

EUROPE.

DESTRUCTION OF THE SPANISH ARMADA.

"The Invincible Armada" — what thoughts crowd upon us at that name of England's later vikings, Sir Francis Drake, Sir John Hawkins, Sir Martin Frobisher and the rest, who returned from the exploration of unknown seas and continents to do brave battle in defence of England's homes and England's faith and liberties!

Philip II., the most powerful monarch of his time, had decreed that England should be subdued and the Protestant religion extinguished, and the wealth and valor and pride of Spain were gathered to do his bidding. With England at his feet the Dutch insurgents could not long hold out, and all of Europe, from the Baltic to the Adriatic, would be ready to do his bidding. France was too weak for rivalry; the dry bones of Germany had not been evoked to life by the summons of a Vasa or a Frederick. Philip was master of the New World, and resolved to dominate the Old. Even the Sultan bowed to his will. England's queen alone, among the leading rulers of Europe, scorned to truckle to the Spaniard, and held aloft the standard of Protestantism.

The Spanish fleet consisted of one hundred and thirty vessels, of greater size than any seen up to that time in Europe. Italy, Portugal and the isles of the Levant contributed to swell the armament, which carried 20,000 soldiers, and was prepared to transport 34,000 more from the Low Countries to invade England. The Spanish vessels resembled castles in their height and hugeness, but their very superiority of size made them unwieldy, and easy prey for the lighter vessels of the English. "They contained within them," we are told, "chambers, chapels, turrets and other commodities of great houses." Their pieces of brazen ordnance were 1600, and of yron a 1000. The bullets thereto belonging were 120,000. Moreover they had great stores of cannons, double cannons, culverings and field-pieces for land services." They had an abundant equipment for the troops in march after landing, and vast quantities of wine, bacon, and other food and drink. "To be short, they brought all things expedient, either for a fleete by sea, or for an armie by land." "This navie was esteemed by the king himselfe to contain 32,000 persons, and to cost him every day 32,000 ducates."

In addition to the Armada, the Duke of

Parma collected a vast flotilla and a squadron of warships at Dunkirk, to transport his army to England, where, under the protection of the Armada the troops were to be landed which were to bring that country under the yoke of Spain.

The English fleet consisted chiefly of merchant vessels gathered from all the ports of the kingdom, while in every part of the country the people armed themselves, and prepared by drilling and soldierly exercises to resist the invaders. The ships of the royal navy numbered thirty-six, but the total number of vessels collected to defend the realm was 191, with 17,472 seamen. The Hollanders came to the assistance of the English with three-score sail, "brave ships of war." Scotland, sore on account of the recent execution of Queen Mary, remained neutral and divided in sympathy, although it was a Scottish mariner named Fleming that gave notice to High Admiral Lord Howard, of the approach of the Armada.

The Armada lay off Calais, the largest ships ranged outside, when the English began the attack, on the night of the twenty-ninth of July, 1588. Eight fire-ships were sent among the Spaniards, causing great confusion, and forcing the Spanish admiral to put to sea. When morning broke the Spaniards ranged themselves near Gravelines. Here the English, with Drake and Fenner in the lead, made a daring and decisive attack on their foes. Says a writer of that day:

"Upon the 29 of July in the morning, the Spanish fleet after the forsayd tumult, having arranged themselues againe into order, were, within sight of Greveling, most bravely and furiously encountered by the English, where they once again got the wind of the Spaniards, who suffered themselues to be deprived of the commodity of the place in Caleis Road, and of the advantage of the wind neer unto Dunkerk, rather than they would change their array or separate their forces now conjoyned and united together standing only upon their defense.

"And albeit there were many excellent and warlike shippes in the English fleet, yet scarce were there 22 or 23 among them all, which matched 90 of the Spanish shippes in the bigness, or could conveniently assault them. Wherefore the English shippes using their prerogative of nimble steerage, whereby they could turn and wield themselues with the wind which way they listed, came often times very near upon the Spaniards, and charged them so sore, that now and then they were but a pike's length asunder; and so continually giving them one broad side after another, they discharged all their shot, both great and small, upon them, spending one whole day, from morning till night, in that violent kind of conflict, untill such time as powder and bullets failed them. In regard of which want they thought it convenient not to pursue the Spaniards any longer, because they had many great vantages of the English, namely, for the extraordinary bigness of their shippes, and also for that they were so neerely conjoyned, and kept together in so good array, that they could by no meanes be fougt withall one to one. The English thought, therefore, that they had right well acquitted themselues in chasing the Spaniards first from Caleis, and then from Dunkerk, and by that means to have hindered them from joyning with the Duke of Parma his forces, and getting the wind of them, to have driven them from their own coasts.

"The Spaniards that day sustained great loss and damage, having many of their shippes shot thorow and thorow, and they discharged likewise great store of ordnance against the English, who, indeed, sustained some hinderance, but not comparable to the Spaniard's loss; for they lost not any one ship or person of account; for very diligent inquisition being made, the Englishmen all that time wherein the Spanish navy sayled upon their seas, are not found to haue wanted aboue one hundred of their people; albeit Sir Francis Drake's ship was pierced with shot aboue forty times, and his very cabben was twice shot thorow, and about the conclusion of the fight, the bed of a certaine gentleman lying weary thereupon, was taken quite from under him with the force of a bullet. Likewise, as the Earle of Northumberland and Sir Charles Blunt were at dinner upon a time, the bullet of a demy-culvering brake thorow the middest of their cabben, touched their feet, and strooke downe two of the standers-by, with many such accidents befalling the English shippes, which it were tedious to rehearse."

The remainder of the defeated Armada, wrote Vice-Admiral Drake, "driven with squibs from their anchors, were chased out of the sight of England, round about Scotland and Ireland; where, for the sympathy of their religion, hoping to find succor and assistance, a great part of them were crushed against the rocks, and those others that landed, being very many in number, were, notwithstanding, broken, slain, and taken, and so sent from village to village, coupled in halters to be shipped into England, where her majesty, of her princely and invincible disposition, disdaining to put them to death, and scorning either to retain or to entertain them, they were all sent back again to their countries, to witness and recount the worthy achievement of their invincible and dreadful navy. Of which the number of soldiers, the fearful burden of their ships, the commanders' names of every squadron, with all others, their magazines of provision, were put in print, as an army and navy irresistible and disdaining prevention; with all which their great and terrible ostentation, they did not in all their sailing round about England so much as sink or take one ship, barque, pinnace, or cock-boat of ours, or even burn so much as one sheep-cote on this land."

Of the Spaniards wrecked on the Irish coast one has handed down a vivid description of his lamentable treatment by those whom he calls "savages." In Scotland the Catholic nobles used their influence in behalf of the fugitives, and secured the safe return of some of them to their native land, instead of being delivered up to the English. The power of Spain was thoroughly humbled, and English adventurers everywhere preyed on her merchantmen and her colonies. English maritime supremacy had its origin in the defeat of the Spanish Armada. The friends of the Reformation everywhere were encouraged to stand firmly for the faith that was in them, and the Dutch were animated also in their glorious struggle for liberty.

PULTOWA.

The Swedish empire, founded by Gustavus Vasa, and extended by his successors over a considerable portion of Europe below the Baltic, was difficult to maintain, and impossible to perpetuate. The Swedes themselves were too few in number to act the part of Romans in vast and subject provinces, separated by a wide sea from the ruling power, and bordered by jealous, hostile and aggressive States. It is one of the plainest lessons of history that contiguous extension is the only extension of empire likely to prove lasting and secure. The annexed provinces grow attached by degrees to their new masters, and distinctions of nationality are gradually effaced and ancient prejudices forgotten. Thus rival kingdoms of the Spanish peninsula were merged in one Spanish monarchy commanding the allegiance alike of Castilian and Andalusian. Thus England, Wales and Scotland became one people, to the common advantage of all. Thus the name of Prussia has become in effect synonymous with that of Germany, or at least of Northern Germany. Thus Russia has spread from the Niemen to the Amoor, and even Austria has held together for centuries its strange mosaic of discordant races.

England, on the other hand, long ago lost her French dominions, on whose conquest and defence so much of English treasure and blood were expended. Spain found the Low Countries only a grave for her armies, and Sweden sacrificed peace and wealth, and the flower of her manhood in a vain effort to keep Germany and Prussia and Poland at her feet.

The ideal, the heroic period of Sweden's military power was when Gustavus Adolphus championed the cause of the suffering Protestants of Germany, and gave up his life on the field of Lutzen in battling for the reformed religion. Germany has never forgotten the great commander who swept down from the North on the hordes of Wallenstein, and died in the hour of victory. Lutzen saved Northern Germany to the Reformation, as the defeat of the Spanish Armada saved England.

"God is my cuirass," said Gustavus Adolphus on the morning of the battle, when his generals urged him to put on armor. At the head of his army he led the charge. The imperial troops fought resolutely, desperately. Sometimes it seemed that the Swedes and their allies would be overwhelmed, but Gustavus, always in the thick of the fight, gave invincible ardor to his followers. Suddenly, in the height of the conflict, as yet undecided, the Swedish king falls, and his riderless horse dashes back into the ranks of the Norsemen.

Not consternation, but a terrible, irresistible determination to save the body of their beloved leader possessed every Swede in that host. With a furious courage that mercenaries could never know, the children of the Vikings swept upon their foes. The host of Wallenstein wavered, then fell back before the almost supernatural onset. The body of the king was rescued, but not before it had been cruelly disfigured with wounds and plundered by the savage Croats. Ten thousand dead and wounded lay on the field, and the artillery of the imperialists fell into the hands of the Swedes and their allies.

Gustavus Adolphus was dead, but able statesmen and gallant soldiers upheld the standard which he had raised, and bore it even to the gates of Vienna. The Peace of Westphalia in 1648, sixteen years after Lutzen, forbade religious persecution, and laid the foundations of modern Germany.

* * * * * *

The battle of Pultowa, about fifty years after the Peace of Westphalia, brought down the always fragile fabric of Swedish empire on the mainland of Europe, and established the power of the Czars. Charles XII., of Sweden, has been called the Madman of the North, but if he had succeded at

Pultowa he would not have been called a madman, and there was even more excuse for his invasion of Russia than for the subsequent enterprise of Napoleon, who had the experience of Charles XII. as a warning. Charles was one of the great commanders of his age, and of all ages. He had military genius of the highest order; he loved war; it was his element, and the completion of one conquest only inspired him to think of another. He was dictator of Europe from the Rhine to the Vistula, with a splendidly equipped army, a country proud of his conquests, and not yet impoverished by his losses, and was courted and feared by every ruler, from Queen Anne to Peter the Czar, when he resolved to invade Muscovy, and dictate terms to the House of Romanoff. Charles was probably actuated in a large degree by desire to punish Peter for his share in the coalition of 1698 against the Swedes, and especially his hypocritical expressions of goodwill while preparing to rob Sweden of its Baltic possessions. Charles would never forgive duplicity. It is certain, whatsoever the underlying motive, that Charles XII. designed to conquer Russia, as he had conquered Poland. There was good reason for his expectation of victory, for he had never failed to defeat the Russians easily in all previous encounters.

King Charles set out from his camp at
Aldstadt, near Leipsic, in September, 1707,
at the head of 45,000 men, and traversed
Poland; 20,000 men, under Count Lewenhaupt, disembarked at Riga and 15,000
were in Finland. "He was therefore in
condition to have brought together 80,000
of the best troops in the world. He left
10,000 men at Warsaw to guard King Stan-
islaus, and in January, 1708, arrived at
Grodno, where he wintered. In June, he
crossed the forest of Minsk, and presented
himself before Borisov; forced the Russian
army, which occupied the left bank of the
Beresina; defeated 20,000 Russians who
were strongly intrenched behind marshes;
passed the Borysthenes at Mohilov, and
vanquished a corps of 16,000 Muscovites
near Smolensko on the 22d of September.
He was now advanced to the confines of
Lithuania, and was about to enter Russia
proper; the Czar, alarmed at his approach,
made him proposals of peace. Up to this
time all his movements were conformable to
rule, and his communications were well
secured. He was master of Poland and
Riga, and only ten days' march distant from
Moscow; and it is probable that he would
have reached that capital, had he not
quitted the high road thither, and directed
his steps toward the Ukraine, in order to
form a junction with Mazeppa, who brought

him only 6000 men. By this movement,
his line of operations, beginning at Sweden,
exposed his flank to Russia for a distance
of four hundred leagues, and he was unable
to protect it, or to receive either reinforcements or assistance."*

The Czar had collected an army of about
100,000 effective men; and though the
Swedes, in the beginning of the invasion,
were successful in every encounter, the
Russian troops were gradually acquiring
discipline; and Peter and his officers were
learning generalship from their victors, as
the Thebans of old learned it from the
Spartans. When Lewenhaupt, in the October of 1708, was striving to join Charles
in the Ukraine, the Czar suddenly attacked
him near the Borysthenes with an overwhelming force of 50,000 Russians. Lewenhaupt fought bravely for three days,
and succeeded in cutting his way through
the enemy with about 4000 of his men to
where Charles awaited him near the River
Desna; but upwards of 8000 Swedes fell in
these battles; Lewenhaupt's cannon and
ammunition were abandoned; and the
whole of his important convoy of provisions,
on which Charles and his half-starved
troops were relying, fell into the enemy's
hands. Charles was compelled to remain

---

* "Napoleon the Great on Charles XII."

in the Ukraine during the winter; but in the spring of 1709 he moved forward toward Moscow, and invested the fortified town of Pultowa, on the River Vorskla; a place where the Czar had stored up large supplies of provisions and military stores, and which commanded the passes leading toward Moscow. The possession of this place would have given Charles the means of supplying all the wants of his suffering army, and would also have furnished him with a secure base of operations for his advance against the Muscovite capital. The siege was therefore hotly pressed by the Swedes; the garrison resisted obstinately; and the Czar, feeling the importance of saving the town, advanced in June to its relief, at the head of an army from fifty to sixty thousand strong.*

Both sovereigns now prepared for the general action, which each saw to be inevitable, and which each felt would be decisive of his own and of his country's destiny. The Czar, by some masterly manœuvres, crossed the Vorskla, and posted his army on the same side of that river with the besiegers, but a little higher up. The Vorskla falls into the Borysthenes about fifteen leagues below Pultowa, and the Czar arranged his forces in two lines,

---

* "Creasy's Fifteen Decisive Battles."

stretching from one river toward the other, so that if the Swedes attacked him and were repulsed, they would be driven backward into the acute angle formed by the two streams at their junction. He fortified these lines with several redoubts, lined with heavy artillery; and his troops, both horse and foot, were in the best possible condition, and amply provided with stores and ammunition. Charles' forces were about 24,000 strong. But no more than half of these were Swedes; so much had battle, famine, fatigue and the deadly frosts of Russia thinned the gallant bands which the Swedish king and Lewenhaupt had led to the Ukraine. The other 12,000 men, under Charles, were Cossacks and Wallachians, who had joined him in the country. On hearing that the Czar was about to attack him, he deemed that his dignity required that he himself should be the assailant; and, leading his army out of their intrenched lines before the town, he advanced with them against the Russian redoubts.

He had been severely wounded in the foot in a skirmish a few days before, and was borne in a litter along the ranks into the thick of the fight. Notwithstanding the fearful disparity of numbers and disadvantage of position, the Swedes never showed their ancient valor more nobly than on that dreadful day. Nor do their Cossack and Wallachian allies seem to have been unworthy of fighting side by side with Charles' veterans. Two of the Russian redoubts were actually entered, and the Swedish infantry began to raise the cry of victory. But, on the other side, neither general nor soldiers flinched in their duty. The Russian cannonade and musketry were kept up; fresh masses of defenders were poured into the fortifications, and at length the exhausted remnants of the Swedish columns recoiled from the blood-stained redoubts. Then the Czar led the infantry and cavalry of his first line outside the works, drew them up steadily and skillfully, and the action was renewed along the whole fronts of the two armies on the open ground. Each sovereign exposed his life freely in the world-winning battle, and on each side the troops fought obstinately and eagerly under their ruler's eyes. It was not till two hours from the commencement of the action that, overpowered by numbers, the hitherto invincible Swedes gave way. All was then hopeless disorder and irreparable rout. Driven downward to where the rivers join, the fugitive Swedes surrendered to their victorious pursuers, or perished in the waters of the Borysthenes. Only a few hundreds swam that river with their king and the Cossack Mazeppa, and escaped into the Turkish territory. Nearly 10,000 lay killed and wounded in the redoubts and on the field of battle.

Sweden never recovered from the blow inflicted at Pultowa, and has never since held rank as a first-class power. Her Baltic provinces fell to Russia, and other antagonists took advantage of Sweden's weakness to share in the spoliation. Sweden was helpless, for about one-fourth of the male population had perished in the wars, and old men and boys alone remained in some of the provinces to cultivate the soil. Russia, on the other hand, went steadily forward in her course of aggrandizement, having disposed of the only enemy she feared.

WATERLOO.

The downfall of Napoleon the Great really dates from the burning of Moscow. The destruction of the grand army which he had led into Russia deprived him of the veterans of Austerlitz and Jena, and left him to fight with conscript regiments against allied Europe, bent on his overthrow, and pledged not to lay down arms until success had been achieved. The young French soldiers fought, it is said, like veterans, but they had opposed to them enemies who felt that Napoleon was no longer invincible, and that his star of em-

pire was on the wane. Between Moscow
and Elba Napoleon achieved some victories
worthy of his fame, but he could not regain
his old ascendency because he no longer
had the resources for war. France was
exhausted; her best soldiers had perished,
and her homes no longer yielded a suffi-
ciency of recruits for the battlefield. Napoleon did not capitulate, however, until
his cause was utterly hopeless, and his capital was in the hands of the enemy.

The Bourbons were responsible for the
Hundred Days. Neither guillotine nor
exile could teach a Bourbon that the world
was moving, and that the France which had
witnessed the Revolution and the Empire
was not the France of Louis XV. The
people, it is true, were no longer offended
by the gross excesses of Versailles and the
Trianon, but Louis XVIII. was a Bourbon
in every fibre. Every day of his reign was
an argument by contrast in favor of the
past with its glories and its sacrifices—and
what will Frenchmen not sacrifice for glory?
The very faults of the absent emperor seemed
brilliant compared with the stolid and worthless respectability of a king who ruled only
by virtue of bayonets steeped in the blood
of France. The French people keenly felt
their degrading position under a sovereign
who was the protege of the very nations
whom French arms had humbled at Auster-

litz, Jena and Friedland. It was a relief to turn their eyes and thoughts to Elba, where sat the idol and the hero of their race.

Napoleon's return found the French people ripe for revolt from their émigré king. The empire was restored far more quickly than it had been overturned, and Napoleon never showed his wonderful genius more signally than in the speed and thoroughness with which he prepared the country to resist the hostile armies which poured toward the frontier with Paris as their goal. Could he have called to life the dry bones of that multitude that had followed him to Russia, of the thousands who had fallen in Germany, on the plains of Lombardy and the hills of Spain, embattled Europe might have met more than its match on the Rhine and in Belgium. But the dead of the Grand Armée could answer the trump no more. The memory of their loyalty, their courage and their sufferings remained a precious legacy to France, but the once invincible battalions would never again align for the charge under the eye of their adored commander. The Old Guard survived, a remnant of the past; but only a remnant.

Napoleon, however, succeeded in gathering an army of about 120,000 men, with a formidable array of artillery, and about 25,000 excellent cavalry. "The whole army was full of ardor," says Count Labèdoyère, "but the emperor, more a slave than could have been credited to recollections and old habits, committed the great fault of replacing his army under the command of its former chiefs, most of whom, notwithstanding their previous addresses to the king, did not cease to pray for the triumph of the imperial cause; yet were not disposed to serve it with that ardor and devotion demanded by imperious circumstances. They were no longer men full of youth and ambition, generously prodigal of their lives to acquire rank and fame; but veterans weary of warfare, who, having attained the summit of promotion, and being enriched by the spoils of the enemy, or the bounty of Napoleon, indulged no other wish than the peaceable enjoyment of their good fortune under the shade of those laurels they had so dearly acquired." The emperor was solemnly warned by Marshal Soult, in behalf of a convention of general officers, against the bestowal on Grouchy of the command of the corps which was to constitute the right flank of Napoleon's army. The emperor did not act on the warning, and Grouchy's failure to support him at Waterloo fully justified the misgivings to which Soult had given expression.

Marshal Blucher had about 116,000 Prussians in Belgium, and the Duke of Wellington commanded about 100,000 men, of whom but a small proportion were British. Napoleon resolved to take his enemies in detail. He defeated the Prussians at Ligny, June 16, 1815, but it was not a crushing defeat. Blucher quickly recovered from the blow, and, reinforced by troops that had not been in the battle, he was prepared to give timely aid to Wellington at Waterloo. Grouchy, detached with 30,000 men by Napoleon to keep the Prussians in check, failed in that object, not through treachery, but incapacity, and spent the remainder of his life explaining why he failed.

The French army at Waterloo amounted to 72,000 men, including about 16,000 cavalry. This did not include the corps under Grouchy, which was detached to observe the Prussians at Wavre. The French artillery numbered 210 pieces. The French infantry was largely composed of "small young men," showing the exhaustion to which incessant conscription had reduced their country. The "Old Guard" were of good physique, and all the French fought well.

The Duke of Wellington had under his command 50,300 infantry, 6950 cavalry and 120 guns. Of the infantry only 17,500 were British, the total effective force of infantry being as follows: British, 17,500; German Legion, 5600; Nassau, 2400; Brunswick, 6400; total, 31,900.

The remainder, composed of Dutch Line

regiments, Pay Bas Line regiments and Dutch militia, were worse than worthless, partly owing to cowardice, and largely, no doubt, to lukewarmness, and secret goodwill toward Napoleon. "They (the Belgians) certainly did not behave well," says Lieutenant-Colonel Tomkinson in his Diary, "and though placed in the second line, and in many instances under cover of the hill, it was difficult to keep them even in that position. When a man was wounded two or three went away with him to the rear. They took great care of their comrades in going off the field, and then commenced plundering in the rear." . . . . .
"There was a regiment of the Pay Bas in square. They were not engaged, nor suffering much from fire, I may say, not in the least cut up whilst I saw them. They were immediately in our front, and fancying the affair rather serious, and that if the enemy advanced any faster (as their fears apprehended) they would have to oppose them, they began firing their muskets in the air, and their rear moved a little, intending under the confusion of their fire and smoke to move off. Major Childers, Eleventh Light Dragoons, and I rode up to them, encouraged them, stopped those who had moved the farthest (ten yards perhaps) out of their ranks, and whilst they were hesitating whether to retreat or continue

with their column the Duke rode up and encouraged them. He said to us, 'That is right, that is right; keep them up.' Childers then brought up his squadron, and by placing it in their rear, they continued steady. Had this one battalion run away at that moment the consequences might have been fatal.'' This extraordinary incident is in itself enough to show the worse than worthless character of the Dutch and Belgian troops at Waterloo. They numbered 18,400 men, and can be counted out altogether as part of the British strength on that day, leaving 31,900 British and German infantry and 6950 British and German cavalry, and 5645 artillerymen, with 156 guns, to oppose Napoleon's army of 48,950 infantry, 15,765 cavalry, 7232 artillerymen and 246 guns. All of Napoleon's troops were animated by one national spirit, they had the bravery common to Frenchmen, and many of them were veterans of his former wars.

The morning of June 18 followed a night of unceasing rain. The British had no tents, and neither officers nor men had a dry garment left to them. Most of them had passed the night without even a fire, and attempts to dry clothing in the morning were made vain by occasional showers. It was a gloomy sky that lowered over the most fateful battlefield of history. "Perhaps those," says Creasy, "who have not seen the field of battle at Waterloo, or the admirable model of the ground and of the conflicting armies which was executed by Captain Siborne, may gain a generally accurate idea of the localities by picturing to themselves a valley, between two or three miles long, of various breadths at different points, but generally not exceeding half a mile. On each side of the valley there is a winding chain of low hills, running somewhat parallel with each other. The declivity from each of these ranges of hills to the intervening valley is gentle but not uniform, the undulations of the ground being frequent and considerable. The English army was posted on the northern, and the French army occupied the southern ridge. The artillery of each side thundered at the other from their respective heights throughout the day, and the charges of horse and foot were made across the valley that has been described. The village of Mont St. Jean is situate a little behind the centre of the northern chain of hills, and the village of La Belle Alliance is close behind the centre of the southern ridge. The high road from Charleroi to Brussels runs through both these villages, and bisects, therefore, both the English and the French positions. The line of this road was the line of Napoleon's intended advance on Brussels.

"The strength of the British position did not consist merely in the occupation of a ridge of high ground. A village and ravine, called Merk Braine, on the Duke of Wellington's extreme right, secured him from his flank being turned on that side; and on his extreme left, two little hamlets, called La Haye and Papillote, gave a similar though a slighter protection. It was, however, less necessary to provide for this extremity of the position, as it was on this (the eastern) side that the Prussians were coming up. Behind the whole British position is the great and extensive forest of Soignies. As no attempt was made by the French to turn either of the English flanks, and the battle was a day of straightforward fighting, it is chiefly important to see what posts there were in front of the British line of hills of which advantage could be taken either to repel or facilitate an attack; and it will be seen that there were two, and that each was of very great importance in the action. In front of the British right, that is to say, on the northern slope of the valley toward its western end, there stood an old-fashioned Flemish farmhouse called Goumont or Hougoumont, with out-buildings and a garden, and with a copse of beech-trees of about two acres in extent around it. This was strongly garrisoned by the allied troops; and while it was in their possession, it was

difficult for the enemy to press on and force
the British right wing. On the other hand,
if the enemy could occupy it, it would be
difficult for that wing to keep its ground on
the heights with a strong post held ad-
versely in its immediate front, being one
that would give much shelter to the enemy's
marksmen, and great facilities for the sudden concentration of attacking columns.
Almost immediately in front of the British
centre, and not so far down the slope as
Hougoumont, there was another farmhouse,
of a smaller size, called La Haye Sainte,
which was also held by the British troops,
and the occupation of which was found to
be of very serious consequence.

"With respect to the French position, the
principal feature to be noticed is the village
of Planchenoit, which lay a little in the rear
of their right (i. e., on the eastern side),
and which proved to be of great importance
in aiding them to check the advance of the
Prussians. The Prussians, on the morning
of the 18th, were at Wavre, about twelve
miles to the east of the field of battle at
Waterloo. The junction of Bulow's division had more than made up for the loss
sustained at Ligny; and leaving Thielman,
with about 17,000 men, to hold his ground
as he best could against the attack which
Grouchy was about to make on Wavre,
Bulow and Blucher moved with the rest of

the Prussians upon Waterloo. It was calculated that they would be there by three o'clock; but the extremely difficult nature of the ground which they had to traverse, rendered worse by the torrents of rain that had just fallen, delayed them long on their twelve miles' march.

"The Duke of Wellington drew up his infantry in two lines, the second line being composed principally of Dutch and Belgian troops, and of those regiments of other nations which had suffered most severely at Quatre Bras on the 16th. The second line was posted on the northern declivity of the hills, so as to be sheltered from the French cannonade. The cavalry was stationed at intervals along the line in the rear, the largest force of horse being collected on the left of the centre, to the east of the Charleroi road. On the opposite heights the French army was drawn up in two general lines, with the entire force of the Imperial Guards, cavalry as well as infantry, in rear of the centre, as a reserve. English military critics have highly eulogized the admirable arrangement which Napoleon made of his forces of each arm, so as to give him the most ample means of sustaining, by an immediate and sufficient support, any attack, from whatever point he might direct it, and of drawing promptly together a strong force, to resist any attack that might be

made on himself in any part of the field.
When his troops were all arrayed, he rode
along the lines, receiving everywhere the
most enthusiastic cheers from his men, of
whose entire devotion to him his assurance
was now doubly sure. On the southern
side of the valley the duke's army was also
arrayed, and ready to meet the menaced
attack.*

"It was approaching noon before the
action commenced. Napoleon, in his
memoirs, gives as the reason for this delay,
the miry state of the ground through the
heavy rain of the preceding night and day,
which rendered it impossible for cavalry or
artillery to manœuvre on it till a few hours
of dry weather had given it its natural con-
sistency. It has been supposed, also, that
he trusted to the effect which the sight of
the imposing array of his own forces was
likely to produce on the part of the allied
army. The Belgian regiments had been
tampered with; and Napoleon had well-
founded hopes of seeing them quit the Duke
of Wellington in a body, and range themselves under his own eagles. The duke,
however, who knew and did not trust them,
had guarded against the risk of this by
breaking up the corps of Belgians, and distributing them in separate regiments among
troops on whom he could rely.

---
*Siborne, quoted by Creasy.

"At last, at about half-past eleven o'clock, Napoleon began the battle by directing a powerful force from his left wing under his brother, Prince Jerome, to attack Hougoumont. Column after column of the French now descended from the west of the southern heights, and assailed that post with fiery valor, which was encountered with the most determined bravery. The French won the copse round the house, but a party of the British Guards held the house itself throughout the day. Amid shell and shot, and the blazing fragments of part of the buildings, this obstinate contest was continued. But still the English held Hougoumont, though the French occasionally moved forward in such numbers as enabled them to surround and mask this post with part of their troops from their left wing, while others pressed onward up the slope and assailed the British right.

"The cannonade, which commenced at first between the British right and the French left, in consequence of the attack on Hougoumont, soon became general along both lines; and about one o'clock Napoleon directed a grand attack to be made under Marshal Ney upon the centre and left wing of the allied army. For this purpose four columns of infantry, amounting to about 18,000 men, were collected, supported by a strong division of cavalry under the celebrated Kellerman, and seventy-four guns were brought forward ready to be posted on the ridge of a little undulation of the ground in the interval between the two main ranges of heights, so as to bring their fire to bear on the British line at a range of about seven hundred yards.

"The columns under Ney descended from the French range of hills, and gained the ridge of the intervening eminence, on which the batteries that supported them were now ranged. As the columns descended again from this eminence, the seventy-four guns opened over their heads with terrible effect upon the troops of the allies that were stationed on the heights to the left of the Charleroi road. One of the French columns kept to the east, and attacked the extreme left of the allies; the other three continued to move rapidly forward upon the left centre of the allied position. The front line of the allies here was composed of Bylant's brigade of Dutch and Belgians. As the French columns moved up the southward slope of the height on which the Dutch and Belgians stood, and the skirmishers in advance began to open their fire, Bylant's entire brigade turned and fled in disgraceful and disorderly panic; but there were men more worthy of the name behind.

"The second line of the allies here consisted of two brigades of English infantry, which had suffered severely at Quatre Bras. But they were under Picton, and not even Ney himself surpassed in resolute bravery that stern and fiery spirit. Picton brought his two brigades forward, side by side, in a thin two-deep line. Thus joined together, they were not 3,000 strong. With these Picton had to make head against the three victorious French columns, upward of four times that strength, and who, encouraged by the easy rout of the Dutch and Belgians, now came confidently over the ridge of the hill. The British infantry stood firm; and as the French halted and began to deploy into line, Picton seized the critical moment: a close and deadly volley was thrown in upon them, and then with a fierce hurrah the British dashed in with the bayonet. The French reeled back in confusion; and as they staggered down the hill, a brigade of the English cavalry rode in on them, cutting them down by whole battalions, and taking 2000 prisoners. The British cavalry galloped forward and sabred the artillerymen of Ney's seventy-four advanced guns; and then cutting the traces and the throats of the horses, rendered these guns totally useless to the French throughout the remainder of the day." Lieutenant-Colonel Tomkins says of this charge: "It was one of the finest ever seen. On going over the

ground the following morning I saw where
two lines of infantry had laid down their
arms; their position was accurately marked
from the regularity the muskets were placed
in. After their success they continued to
advance, and moved forward in scattered
parties up to the reserve of the enemy, and
to the top nearly of the heights held by
them. In this scattered state they were
attacked by a heavy brigade of cavalry.
They were obliged to retreat. . . . .
The loss of the second brigade was immense,
and the more to be regretted, for had they
halted after completely routing the enemy's
troops their loss would have been trifling,
and the brigade remained efficient for the
rest of the day." In this charge Sir
Thomas Picton was killed at the head of
his squadron, and Sir William Ponsonby at
the head of his brigade.

The French continued to charge in vain
the stubborn ranks of the British, and while
the losses of the latter were terrible, those
of the French were greater. "Whenever
the enemy made an attack," says Lieutenant-Colonel Tomkinson, "they covered it
with all the artillery they could thunder at
us, and we again worked their columns in
advancing with every gun we could bring
against them. One brigade of guns was
firing at a brigade of the enemy's which
had got their range and annoyed them.

They were ordered by the duke not to fire at the enemy's guns, but to direct all shot against their columns. We might run a chance of losing the position from a severe attack of one of their columns, but could not by their cannonade. The manner their columns were cut up in making the attack was extraordinary, and the excellence of practice in artillery was never exceeded. The enemy fired a great deal, yet at times I thought rather wildly."

Meantime Napoleon knew that over his army hung the dark shadow of the forces under Blucher and Bulow. These forces attacked the rear of the French right about half-past four in the afternoon, but were driven back and kept at bay after fierce fighting, in which thousands fell. Nevertheless, they kept a corps of the French army engaged; other Prussians were approaching, and Napoleon saw that he must crush Wellington quickly, or his cause was lost. Night was approaching when the final charge was made—that charge upon the result of which depended the fate of Europe. The infantry of the Old Guard was formed in two columns, and Ney led the advance, while a fearful fire of artillery sent shell and round shot and grapeshot swept from the French batteries through the British and Anglo-German ranks. These stood the blast of death with a heroism never surpassed on the battlefield, the Duke of Wellington himself being foremost in leading and urging his men. For a brief time the issue seemed doubtful; the French gained some ground, and thought they were dashing on to certain victory, when suddenly, with the enemy within fifty yards, the Duke of Wellington called: "Up Guards, and at them!"

Four feet deep uprose the British line, and poured a deadly volley into the French. Hundreds of Napoleon's veterans fell dead and wounded, and the rest were thrown into disorder. Volley followed volley, and then came the bayonet charge. The French fled. Waterloo was won. The Prussian share of the battle was that of wolves on the wounded lion. Germans did glorious work at Waterloo, but they were the Germans who served under Wellington. The credit of winning the battle of Waterloo is due to British pluck and endurance. The French found the British very different from the enemies they had been accustomed to meet. Lieutenant-Colonel Tomkinson says on this subject: "This is the system they have gone upon with every other nation, and have succeeded. They move an overawing column or two to one point. It comes up with the greatest regularity, and on arriving at close quarters with their opponents they carry so steady and determined an appearance that those hitherto opposed to them have generally abandoned their positions without being beaten out of them." The French found that the British were made of sterner stuff, as indeed they ought to have known from experience in the Peninsula.

In the battle of Waterloo the troops under the Duke of Wellington lost 16,186 men, and the Prussians 6999, making a total loss for the allies of 23,185 men. The French lost 18,500 killed and wounded, and 7800 captured. It is worthy of note that the losses might have been much heavier but for the rain of the previous night. The effect of the rain was to make the ground so wet that shells often sank into the soil where they fell, and did little or no injury, and the same was the case with round-shot.

KONIGGRATZ.

Koniggratz was made inevitable by the growth of the Prussian monarchy, and the consequent rivalry between Prussia and Austria for predominance in Germany. The Schleswig-Holstein difficulty was merely the occasion, the incident, the match that in the hand of Prince Bismarck lighted the fire of war. "One single encounter, one decisive battle," said Bismarck in 1865, "and Prussia will have it in her power to dictate conditions." The Convention of

Gastein postponed the struggle for a few months, although King William of Prussia had hoped that it would lead to permanent peace. Bismarck knew better. He continued his plans for war, and artfully induced Louis Napoleon to remain passive in the approaching conflict by playing upon his dream of Italy's liberation—the one redeeming feature in Louis Napoleon's character and reign. The Schleswig-Holstein difference was fostered; the relations between Prussia and Austria became more and more embittered, and at length the two powers began advancing troops toward the frontier. Italy, too, began to arm as an ally of Prussia, and Austria was confronted by two enemies instead of one. For Italy the Austrians had only contempt, in some degree justified by subsequent events, but hostilities in the South made more serious and difficult the problem in the North.

Prussia also had foes on her flanks. Hanover, Saxony and Hesse-Cassel still dared to dispute the supremacy of Berlin, and were in avowed sympathy with Austria. Bismarck did not hesitate in dealing with these lesser antagonists. Prussian troops occupied the capitals of the States named, and started in pursuit of their armies. The Hanoverians fought gallantly at Laugensalza, but were compelled to surrender to King William. The Hessian army hastened to make junction with the "army of the South," a Bavarian corps 40,000 strong, and another corps of 46,000 drawn from Wurtemberg, Baden, Hesse-Darmstadt and Nassau. These troops, poorly organized, and ill-prepared to meet the thoroughly trained forces of King William, were beaten in detail by Generals Vogel von Falckenstein and Manteuffel, with numbers about half as strong as their opponents. The Saxon army of 30,000 took the only effective course by marching into Bohemia and joining the Austrians under Benedek.

King William was in supreme command of the Prussian forces, which consisted of three separate armies; the first in the centre, of about 100,000 men, led by Prince Frederick Charles, the king's nephew, and called the "Army of Bohemia;" the second, on the left, called the "Army of Silesia," and numbering 116,000 men, under the Crown Prince, afterward Emperor Frederick, and the third or "Army of the Elbe," on the right, composed of 40,000 men, commanded by Herwarth von Bittenfeld.

It was the shortest great war in history. Although the Austrians had been preparing, the Prussians virtually took them by surprise, and assailed them with far superior forces. Battle after battle was won by the Prussians, and at length the two great armies confronted each other, July 2, 1866,

near the town of Koniggratz. The king
held a council of war, and it was resolved
to let the troops rest on the following day,
and get ready to strike a crushing blow.
Meantime, however, it was learned that the
Austrians were arranging to attack, and at
midnight the old king called another council, and it was determined not to wait for
the enemy, but to strike at dawn of day.

Prince Frederick Charles, with his three
corps, was to assail Benedek with his five
corps, while Herwarth von Bittenfeld should
fall upon the left flank of the Austrians,
and the Crown Prince attack their right.
When this plan was decided upon the
Crown Prince was more than twenty miles
away, and it was four o'clock in the morning when the courier arrived at his quarters
with the order from the king. He pledged
himself to do his part in the battle, and his
royal father felt full confidence that the son
would keep his word. The battle did not
begin, however, until about eight o'clock,
when Frederick Charles, amid a pouring
rain, opened his guns on the Austrians.

The king, with Bismarck and his staff
appeared among the troops, and the thunderous cheers which greeted them showed
the loyal and confident spirit of the soldiers.
Through long hours of that gloomy day the
cannon thundered, and the Prussian needle-
gun sent rapid death among Austria's bat-

talions, but the latter remained unbroken, and the struggle so far indecisive, while the king and his generals looked anxiously for the coming of the Crown Prince. "Suddenly Bismarck lowered his glass, and drew the attention of his neighbors to certain lines in the far distance. All telescopes were pointed thither, but the lines were pronounced to be furrows. 'These are not furrows,' said Bismarck, after another scrutinizing look; 'the spaces are not equal; they are advancing lines.' And so they were; and soon thereafter the cannon-thunder of 'Unser Fritz,' with the irresistible rush of the Guards up the heights of Chlune and Kosberitz brought relief and joy to the minds of all."*

Attacked now on both flanks, and the centre unable to hold its own against renewed and overwhelming assault, the Austrians gave way, and retreat soon became a disordered rout. King William led forward the cavalry reserve of the first army, which met and scattered the Austrian cavalry reserve. From the opening to the close of the battle which he thus brought to a triumphant ending, King William never avoided danger. Shells shrieked by his head, men were struck down around him, but he remained as exposed and indifferent

---

*Love's "Prince Bismarck."

to the perils of battle as the bravest of his troopers. "To my repeated request," says Bismarck, "that His Majesty might not so carelessly expose himself to so murderous a fire he only answered, 'The commander-in-chief must be where he ought to be.'"

The number of men engaged at Koniggratz was, according to Captain Otto Benndt's recent work on "Warfare in Figures," 436,000, of whom about 230,000 were Prussians. The Austrian force included 30,000 Saxons. The Prussians had 800 guns and the Austrians nearly the same number. The Prussians lost about 10,000 killed and wounded, and the Austrians 40,000, of whom 18,000 were prisoners, together with 11 standards and 174 guns. Even Bismarck was touched by the awful spectacle of the battlefield, with its 32,000 of dead and dying and wounded. "I have lost all except, alas, my life," exclaimed Marshal Benedek, the Austrian commander.

Austria, by the Treaty of Prague, agreed to a Prussian annexation of Schleswig-Holstein, Hanover, Hesse-Cassel and Nassau, and the free city of Frankfort. Bismarck, upon an earnest appeal from France, consented to forego the annexation of Saxony, that kingdom agreeing to join the Confederation of the North. Prussia, without Saxony, acquired territories which added four and a half millions to her population, and increased her area by about a fourth of its previous extent. Bavaria and Hesse were required to pay an indemnity of thirty and three millions of gulden respectively, and Wurtemberg and Baden were severally fined eight and six millions of gulden for their share in the hostilities against Prussia.* These easy terms for the South German States are in part accounted for by their agreement to sign secret treaties conferring the command of their several armies on the King of Prussia in the event of a foreign attack upon Germany. Bismarck also weighed the fact that the annexation of the South German States to Prussia would bring in an element not easily assimilated, and likely to prove a source of weakness instead of strength, whereas, permitted to retain independence, the South Germans would be useful and valuable allies in the next movement toward German unification.

The Treaty of Prague made Austria a power alien to Germany, although the dominant element in Austria is German. From the day of the Koniggratz defeat Austria turned her gaze more than ever toward the Balkans, and she has made up to some extent by gains in that direction for losses in Germany and Italy.

---

*The gulden of the South German States at the time of the treaty of Prague was worth about 35 cents.

The Italians were rewarded for good intentions and poor performance by the cession of Venetia. Not until 1870, however, after Sedan, was the unity of Italy made complete by the surrender of Rome.

SEDAN.

Prussia did not provoke the Franco-German war, but she was ready for it, and she welcomed it. Bismarck had long foreseen that only war with France could rivet that German unity upon which he had set his heart, and to the accomplishment of which he devoted his existence. France still affected to treat Prussia as an inferior instead of an equal, and neither France nor Germany had forgotten that Ligny was the final victory of the First Napoleon, and that Prussia had no triumph to her credit to offset that memorable defeat. Even the success of Prussia in her war with Austria had not diminished the arrogance of France, although it had made the French emperor more cautious for the time being in his attitude toward his German neighbors.

In 1870, Louis Napoleon believed that his armies were in a condition to repeat his uncle's march to Berlin, but, unlike the great Napoleon, he acted on the information of others, and was thoroughly deceived. He did not have half the force at his command that he supposed, and when it came to actual warfare the Germans were able to present two soldiers for every Frenchman in the field. The German military system was a perfect machine, and its commissariat in admirable order; whereas the French was dry-rotted with corruption, and inefficient in every department. But for the courage of which the French gave heroic illustration amid the most depressing circumstances, the French side of the Franco-German war would have been the most disgraceful exhibition of military incompetency on the part of a great nation within the present century.

War was declared by France July 19, 1870. Within two weeks Germany had over one million of men ready for the conflict, and half a million or more on the march for the Rhine. At their head was King William, venerable in years but as brave and ready for the field as the youngest man in his host. With him went Bismarck, the statesman, and Von Moltke, the greatest warrior of them all, a master of military tactics, the Grant and the Lee of Europe. "March separately—strike combined"—is said to have been Von Moltke's motto, and he carried it out thoroughly in the swift and terrific campaign of 1870. Moving vast armies along separate routes—thus facilitating their march, and making their sustenance the easier, the German commanders always presented a largely superior force in actual conflict, and although in almost every battle their losses considerably exceeded those of the French, they could readily replenish the vacant ranks, and still have the advantage of superior numbers.

The Franco-German war was an advance on the part of the Germans from one field of slaughter to another. Every stand which the French made marked a German victory, usually won at a far greater cost of life to the victors than to the vanquished. But for one German that fell in battle, ten poured across the frontier.

The first serious conflict of the war took place on August 4, at Weissenburg, where the German advance-guard was attacked by the French under General Douay. The French commander was killed, and his troops driven back in disorder. On August 6, General Steinmetz, with 120,000 Germans, fought a bloody battle at Spicheren with 60,000 French, led by General Frossard. The French were defeated, with a loss of about 4000 dead and wounded, and 2500 prisoners. The German loss in dead and wounded was also about 4000. On the same day the Crown Prince Frederick defeated MacMahon at Woerth, taking 6000 prisoners, 6 mitrailleuses and 35 cannon.

Both wings of the French army having met with disaster, the original position could no longer be held, and the different corps gathered into two large masses to retreat along the line of the Moselle. Two different armies were thus formed—the Army of Metz, commanded by Marshal Bazaine, and the Army of Chalons, commanded by Marshal MacMahon.

On August 14, the Germans, 80,000 strong, attacked the French, 60,000 in number, near Metz, and after a sanguinary struggle, in which the Germans lost between 4000 and 5000 killed and wounded, the French were compelled to retire into the fortifications. On August 16, the battle of Mars-la-Tour was fought at which the entire French army of the Rhine was repulsed by Prince Frederick Charles, and driven back on Gravelotte, the Germans, however, suffering immense loss. At Gravelotte, on August 18, occurred the greatest battle of the war, in which 280,000 Germans were arrayed against 160,000 Frenchmen. The French army occupied a very strong position to the west of Metz, but after nine hours of a fiercely contested conflict, with terrible slaughter on both sides, the French were completely routed, cut off from their communications with Paris and forced back toward Metz. The French lost 609 officers and 11,605 men; the Germans, 904 officers and 19,658 men. The French army, under Bazaine, was now shut up in the fortress of Metz.

On Tuesday, the 30th of August, the army of the Crown Prince overtook MacMahon's corps a short distance north of Rheims; and after a fierce battle, of enormous slaughter on each side, the Prussians drove the shattered army of the French in utter rout towards Sedan. During all the hours of the 31st, the battle raged in an incessant series of bloody skirmishes, as the French troops, about a hundred thousand in number, pressed on every side, fell back, bleeding, exhausted, despairing, into Sedan.

The dawn of the morning of the 1st of September found the French so surrounded as to be cut off from all possibility of retreat. They were crowded together in a narrow space, while five hundred pieces of artillery were opening fire upon them. At five o'clock in the morning, the terrific storm of battle opened its thunders. It was an awful day. In the first hour of the battle, General MacMahon was struck by the splinter of a shell, and was carried back, severely wounded, into Sedan. The command passed to General Wimpffen. Nearly three hundred thousand men were now hurling a storm of bullets, shot and shell into the crowded ranks of the French.

It was an indescribable scene of tumult and carnage. A correspondent of one of the London papers writes:

"All describe the conduct of the emperor as that of one who either cared not for death, or actually threw himself in its way. In the midst of the scene of confusion which ensued upon the irruption of the panic-stricken French into Sedan, the emperor, riding slowly through a wide street swept by the German artillery and choked by the disordered soldiery, paused a moment to address a question to a colonel of his staff.

"At the same instant a shell exploded a few feet in front of Napoleon, leaving him unharmed; though it was evident to all around that he had escaped by a miracle. The emperor continued on his way without manifesting the slightest emotion, greeted by the enthusiastic *vivats* of the troops. Later, while sitting at a window inditing his celebrated letter to the King of Prussia, a shell struck the wall just outside, and burst only a few feet from the emperor's chair, again leaving him unscathed and unmoved."

For five hours the emperor had been exposed to a fire which filled the air with bullets, ploughed up the ground at his feet, and covered the field with the mutilated and the dead. At half-past three o'clock in the afternoon, General Wimpffen sent an officer to propose that the emperor should place himself in the middle of a column of men who should endeavor to cut their way through the enemy. The emperor replied that he could not consent to save himself at the sacrifice of so many men; that he had determined to share the fate of the army. Though a large portion of the army was still fighting valiantly upon the heights around the walls, the streets of Sedan were choked with the debris of all the corps, and were fiercely bombarded from all sides.

After twelve hours of so unequal a conflict, the commanders of the *corps d'armée* reported to the emperor that they could no longer offer any serious resistance. The emperor ordered the white flag to be raised upon the citadel, and sent the following letter to his Prussian Majesty, who was with the conquering army:—

"Sire, my brother, not having been able to die in the midst of my troops, it only remains for me to place my sword in the hands of your Majesty.

"I am of your Majesty the good brother,
"NAPOLEON."

William immediately replied, "Sire, my brother, regretting the circumstances under which we meet, I accept this word of your Majesty; and I pray you to name one of your officers provided with full powers to treat for the capitulation of the army which has so bravely fought under your command. On my side, I have named General Moltke for this purpose.

"I am of your Majesty the good brother,
"WILLIAM."

General Wimpffen was sent to the Prussian headquarters. "Your army," said General Moltke, "does not number more than eighty thousand men. We have two hundred and thirty thousand, who completely surround you. Our artillery is everywhere in position, and can destroy the place in two hours. You have provisions for only one day, and scarcely any more ammunition. The prolongation of your defence would be only a useless massacre."

General Wimpffen returned to Sedan. A council of thirty-two generals was called. With but two dissentient voices, it was decided to be useless to sacrifice any more lives. The capitulation was signed.

King William, in a letter which he wrote to Queen Augusta, speaks as follows of his fallen foes:—

"You already know, through my three telegrams, the extent of the great historical event which has just happened. It is like a dream, though one has seen it unroll itself hour after hour. On the morning of the 2d I drove to the battlefield, and met Moltke, who was coming to obtain my consent to the capitulation. He told me that the emperor had left Sedan at five o'clock, and had come to Donchery. As he wished to speak to me, and there was a chateau in the neighborhood, I chose this for our meeting. At one o'clock I started with Fritz, escorted by the cavalry staff. I alighted before the chateau, where the emperor came to meet me. We were both much moved at meeting again under such circumstances. What my feelings were, considering that I had seen Napoleon only three years before at the summit of his power, is more than I can describe."

The illustrious captive was assigned to the Castle of Wilhelmshohe, near Cassel, one of the most attractive castles in Germany. Accompanied by his friends, supplied with every comfort, and surrounded by a guard of honor, the chains which held the prisoner of war were invisible.

The tidings of this great calamity soon reached Paris, and created intense excitement.

The second French empire was at an end, and the proclamation of King William of Prussia as German emperor, at Versailles, in December, 1870, crowned the great task of Bismarck's life. In France a real republic arose from the ruins of the empire and the ashes of the Commune, and the French nation is now in a more prosperous condition, and better provided with all the elements that contribute to it, than at any time in its past history.

AMERICA.

DUQUESNE.

The closing years of the seventeenth century witnessed the beginning of the struggle between France and England for empire in North America. Marquette, Joliet and La Salle won for France by daring exploration a nominal title to the Mississippi Valley, and La Salle assumed possession of the great river and its country in the name of Louis XIV., after whom he called the region Louisiana. It was a vast dominion indeed that was thus claimed for the House of Bourbon without a settlement and with hardly an outpost to make any real show of sovereignty. Even had the expulsion of James II. from the English throne not hastened an outbreak between England and France, the conflict would have been inevitable. The war began in 1689, and with intervals of peace and sometimes in spite of peace the contest continued, until 1763, with varying fortunes, but ultimately resulting in the complete overthrow of the French.

* * * * * * *

The point of land where the Allegheny and Monongahela meet in turbulent eddies and form the Beautiful River, early engaged the attention of the two nations, rivals for the dominion of the northern continent, while between two of the leading British colonies grave difference existed as to ownership of the coveted territory. Pennsylvania, held in leading strings by a Quaker policy which endeavored to reconcile the savage realities of an age of iron with theories of a golden millennium, failed to sustain her assertion of right with the energies that her population and resources might well have commanded, and Virginia, more ambitious and militant, boldly pushed an armed expedition into the very heart of the border wilderness, and began with the attack on Jumonville and his party the war that ended on the Plains of Abraham.

In 1750 the Ohio Company, formed for the purpose of colonizing the country on the river of that name, surveyed its banks as far as the site of Louisville. The French, resolved to defend their title to the region west of the mountains, crossed Lake Erie, and established posts at Presque Isle, at Le Boeuf, and at Venango on the Allegheny River. Governor Dinwiddie, of Virginia, sent a messenger to warn the French not to advance. He selected for this task a young man named George Washington, a land surveyor, who, notwithstanding his youth, had made a good impression as a person of capacity and courage, well-fitted for the arduous and delicate undertaking. Washington well performed his task, although the French, as might have been expected, paid no heed to his warning. In the spring of 1754, a party of English began to build a fort where Pittsburg now stands. The French drove them off and erected Fort Duquesne. A regiment of Virginia troops was already marching toward the place. Upon the death of its leading officer, George Washington, the lieutenant-colonel, took command. Washington, overwhelmed by the superior numbers of the French, was compelled to surrender, and the French, for the first time, were masters of the Ohio.

This reverse did not diminish the esteem in which Washington was held by the Virginians, and by those of the mother country who came in contact with him. When General Edward Braddock, in 1755, started on his ill-fated expedition for the capture of Duquesne with a force of about two thousand men, including the British regulars and the colonial militia, Washington

accompanied the British general as one of
his staff. Braddock was a gallant soldier,
but imperious and self-willed, and he looked
almost with contempt upon the American
troops. He made a forced march with
twelve hundred men in order to surprise
the French at Duquesne before they could
receive reinforcements. Colonel Dunbar
followed with the remainder of the army
and the wagon train.

It was a delightful July morning when
the British soldiers and colonists crossed a
ford of the Monongahela, and advanced in
solid platoons along the southern bank of
the stream in the direction of the fort.
Washington advised a disposition of the
troops more in accordance with forest warfare, but Braddock haughtily rejected the
advice of the "provincial colonel," as he
called Washington. The army moved on,
recrossed the river to the north side, and
continued the march to Duquesne. The
news of the British advance had been carried to the fort by Indian scouts. The
French at first thought of abandoning the
post, but they decided to attack the British
with the aid of Indian allies. De Beaujeu
led the French and Indians. The British
were proceeding in fancied security when
the forest rang with Indian yells, and a
volley of bullets and flying arrows dealt
death in their ranks. The regular troops

were thrown into confusion, and Braddock tried courageously to rally them. Washington showed the admirable qualities which afterward made him victor in the Revolution. Cool and fearless amid the frantic shouts of the foe and the panic of the British soldiery, he gave Braddock invaluable assistance in endeavoring to retrieve the fortunes of the day. The provincials fought frontier fashion, nearly all losing their lives, but not without picking off many of their enemies. Beaujeu, the French commander, was killed in the opening of the engagement.

Of eighty-six English officers sixty-three were killed or wounded; and about one-half the private soldiers fell, while a number were made prisoners. For two hours the battle raged, until Braddock, having had five horses shot under him, went down himself, mortally wounded. Then the regulars that remained took flight, and Washington, left in command, ordered a retreat, carrying with him his dying general. Braddock died three days after the battle, expressing regret that he had not followed the counsel of Washington. The British prisoners were taken to Duquesne, and that evening the Indians lighted fires on the banks of the Allegheny River, near the fort, and tortured the captives to death. An English boy who was a prisoner at Duquesne, having been previously captured, and who afterward related his experience in a narrative, a copy of which the writer has examined, says that the cries of the victims could be heard in the fort. The boy himself was subjected to closer confinement than usual, apparently for fear that the savages might demand that he be given up to them.

The French continued to win battles, until a master hand seized the helm in Great Britain. William Pitt, the "Great Commoner," determined upon a vigorous prosecution of the war in America. General John Forbes was sent in 1758, with about nine thousand men to reduce Fort Duquesne. The illness which caused his death in the following year may be fairly accepted in excuse and explanation of the incompetent management of the expedition, and its almost fatal delays. Fortunately the French appeared to have lost the vigor and daring which they had displayed in the defeat of Braddock, and the sullen roar of an explosion, when the British troops were within a few miles of Duquesne, gave notice that it had been abandoned without a blow. General Forbes changed the name of the place to Fort Pitt, in honor of that illustrious minister to whose energetic direction of affairs was largely due the expulsion of the French arms from North America.

When Westminster Abbey shall have crumbled over the tombs of Britain's heroes, and the House of Hanover shall have joined the misty dynasties of the past, Pittsburg will remain a monument, growing in grandeur with the progress of ages, to England's great statesman of the eighteenth century.

The French never returned to the forks of the Ohio. From the hour of their retreat from Duquesne they gave up step by step to the British, until the battle of the Plains of Abraham put an end to the once magnificent dream of a greater France in the New World.

SARATOGA.

The disastrous campaign of General Sir John Burgoyne in the summer of 1777 against Northern New York was the turning-point of the American Revolution. The object of the invasion was to seize the Hudson River, and divide the colonies by a continuous British line from Canada to the city of New York. Had the plan succeeded it would have been an almost fatal blow to the cause of independence. Its failure was not due to the courage or skill of any one American commander, but to the indomitable resolution with which every step of the invading army was resisted by Americans of every rank. The whole country rose as one man to oppose and harass the enemy, and it seemed as if every militiaman understood that the fate of his country depended on the repulse or destruction of the foe.

Burgoyne's plan of campaign, as concerted with the British ministry, was to march to Albany with a large force by way of Lakes Champlain and George, while another force under Sir Henry Clinton advanced up the Hudson. At the same time Colonel Barry St. Leger was to make a diversion by way of Oswego, on the Mohawk River. Burgoyne began his advance in June, with about eight thousand men. Proceeding up Lake Champlain he compelled the Americans to evacuate Crown Point, Ticonderoga and Fort Anne. His first blunder was in failing to avail himself of the water carriage of Lake George, at the head of which there was a direct road to Fort Edward. Instead of taking this course he spent three weeks in cutting a road through the woods, and building bridges over swamps. This gave time for General Schuyler to gather the yeomanry in arms, and for Washington to send troops from the southern department to reinforce Schuyler. Burgoyne also lost valuable time in a disastrous attack on Bennington.

Burgoyne issued a proclamation in most bombastic style. In the preamble he stated, besides his military and other distinctions, that he was "author of a celebrated tragic comedy called the 'Blockade of Boston.'" He accused the patriots of enormities "unprecedented in the inquisitions of the Romish Church," and offered to give encouragement, employment and assistance to all who would aid the side of the king. "I have but to give stretch," he concluded, "to the Indian forces under my direction—and they amount to thousands—to overtake the hardened enemies of Great Britain and America. I consider them the same wherever they lurk. If notwithstanding these endeavors and sincere inclination to assist them the frenzy of hostility should remain, I trust I shall stand acquitted in the eyes of God and of men in denouncing and executing the vengeance of the State against the willful outcasts. The messengers of justice and of wrath await them in the field, and devastation, famine and every concomitant horror that a reluctant but indispensable prosecution of military duty must occasion will bar the way to their return."

While Burgoyne's army was lying near Fort Edward occurred the tragic death of Jane McCrea, celebrated in song and story. Jane was the second daughter of the Reverend James McCrea, a Presbyterian clergyman of Scottish descent, and she made her home with her brother, John, at Fort Edward, New York. John McCrea was a patriot, but Jane had for her lover an officer in Burgoyne's army named David Jones, to whom she was betrothed. Between John McCrea and David Jones an estrangement had arisen on account of their opposite political sympathies, but Jane clung to her affianced. "My dear Jenny," wrote Jones, under date of July 11, 1777, "these are sad times, but I think the war will end this year, as the rebels cannot hold out, and will see their error. By the blessing of Providence I trust we shall yet pass many years together in peace. . . . . No more at present, but believe me yours affectionately till death." How faithfully he kept that promise!

Jane McCrea well deserved her lover's devotion. She is described as a young woman of rare accomplishments, great personal attractions, and of a remarkable sweetness of disposition.* She was of medium stature, finely formed, of a delicate blonde complexion. Her hair was of a golden brown and silken lustre, and when unbound trailed upon the ground. Her father was devoted to literary pursuits, and she thus had acquired a taste for reading, unusual in one of her age—about twenty-four years—in those early times.

---

*See "The Burgoyne Ballads." by William L. Stone, from whose narrative this sketch is taken.

When Burgoyne's army was about four miles from Fort Edward, David Jones sent a party of Indians, under Duluth, a half-breed, to escort his betrothed to the British camp, where they were to be married at once by Chaplain Brudenell, Lady Harriet Acland and Madame Riedesel, wife of General Riedesel, in command of the Brunswick contingent, having consented to be present at the wedding. It had been arranged that Duluth should halt in the woods about a quarter of a mile from the house of a Mrs. McNeil where Jane was waiting to join him at the appointed time. Meanwhile it happened that a fierce Wyandotte chief named Le Loup, with a band of marauding Indians from the British camp, drove in a scouting party of Americans, and stopping on their return from the pursuit at Mrs. McNeil's house, took her and Jane captive, with the intention of taking them to the British camp. On their way back Le Loup and his followers encountered Duluth and his party. The half-breed stated his errand and demanded that Jane be given up to him. Le Loup insisted on escorting her. Angry words followed and Le Loup, in violent passion, shot Jane through the heart. Then the savage tore the scalp from his victim and carried it to the British camp. Mrs. McNeil had arrived at the camp a little in advance, having been separated from Jane before the tragedy. She at once recognized the beautiful tresses. David Jones never recovered from the shock. It is said that he was so crushed by the terrible blow, and disgusted with the apathy of Burgoyne in refusing to punish the miscreant who brought the scalp of Jane McCrea to the camp as a trophy, claiming the bounty offered for such prizes by the British, that he asked for a discharge and upon this being refused deserted, having first rescued the precious relic of his beloved from the savages. Jones retired to the Canadian wilderness, and spent the remainder of his life unmarried, a silent and melancholy man.

The murder of Jane McCrea fired New York. From every farm, from every village, from every cabin in the woods the men of America thronged to avenge her death. Her name was a rallying cry along the banks of the Hudson and in the mountains of Vermont, and "her death contributed in no slight degree to Burgoyne's defeat, which became a precursor and principal cause of American independence."*

The force of about two thousand men, whom Colonel Barry St. Leger led into the forests of what is now Oneida County, met stout resistance, and but for the Indian allies of the British, led by the great Mo-

---
*Stone, "The Burgoyne Ballads."

hawk chief, Joseph Brant, St. Leger's troops would probably have been destroyed or made captive. The fierce battle of Oriskany, in which the brave General Herkimer received a fatal wound, was a patriot victory, but it gave St. Leger a respite. When he heard that Benedict Arnold was approaching with troops sent by General Schuyler, to give him battle, he retreated to Lake Ontario, shattering Burgoyne's hopes of aid from the Tories of the Mohawk Valley. Meanwhile Congress had relieved General Schuyler from command in the North, and appointed Horatio Gates in his place. Gates was not a man of ability, but he was ably seconded in his operations against Burgoyne by Benedict Arnold.

General Howe had intended to take Philadelphia and then co-operate with Burgoyne in inflicting a final and crushing blow on the Americans, but the Fabian strategy of Washington again proved too much for the British. Howe being prevented by Washington from crossing New Jersey with his army, undertook an expedition by sea. He sailed up Chesapeake Bay, marched northward with 18,000 men to Brandywine Creek, and there met Washington with 11,000, on the eleventh of September. The British held the field, but Washington retreated slowly, disputing

every foot of ground, and it was not until
the twenty-sixth of September that Howe
entered Philadelphia. Washington attacked
the British encampment at Germantown at
daybreak on the fourth of October, and
attempted to drive the British into the
Schuylkill River. One American battalion
fired into another by mistake, and this unhappy accident probably saved the British
from another Trenton on a larger scale.
Howe was unable to send any assistance to
Burgoyne until it was too late to save that
commander.

Burgoyne found his progress stopped by
the intrenchments of the Americans under
General Gates, at Bemis Heights, nine
miles south of Saratoga, and he endeavored
to extricate himself from his perilous position by fighting.

On September 19, Burgoyne attacked the
American lines. The patriots were well
prepared to receive him. General Benedict
Arnold, who commanded the American left,
did not wait for the enemy to come, but
having approached under cover of the
woods, charged furiously on Burgoyne's
centre. The battle raged fiercely for about
four hours, Arnold displaying the most
reckless bravery, in marked contrast to the
cautious policy of his superior, General
Gates. The American troops were animated by their leader's example, and

astonished the British by the desperate courage with which they disputed the ground. At length, under cover of darkness, the Americans drew off, after killing and wounding 600 of the 3500 British. The American loss was much less, and although Burgoyne held the field he realized that another conflict with similar havoc would be the ruin of himself and his army. He looked anxiously for the reinforcements which did not come.

On the seventh of October the British, with their Tory and Indian allies, moved forward to another attack. This time the Americans were better prepared, and made stronger than on the first day's battle. They rushed upon Burgoyne's lines, and the Germans and the grenadiers gave way before the impetuous charge. General Simon Fraser, the best, and one of the bravest of Burgoyne's officers, was shot dead while attempting to cover the retreat. Fearing danger to his own lines Burgoyne abandoned the field, leaving six cannon to the victors, and many dead and wounded. Benedict Arnold followed in a headlong charge upon the British intrenchments. His horse was shot under him, and he was wounded in the leg; but he broke through the British lines, and held out against all attacks. Burgoyne abandoned his lines that night, and occupied a new position.

The fate of his army was now sealed. He
was cut off from assistance, and at the
mercy of Gates. The funeral of General
Fraser, under these melancholy circumstances, was a peculiarly sad celebration.

On October 16, a convention was signed
by the terms of which Burgoyne surrendered
his entire army to the Americans. The
force surrendered numbered 5763 men, and
included two lieutenant-generals, two major-
generals and three brigadier-generals. The
ordnance, part of which had previously
been taken in battle by the Americans, consisted of thirty-eight pieces of light artillery attached to columns, six twenty-four
pounders, six twelve-pounders and four
howitzers.

The surrender of Burgoyne gave to the
American cause a status which it had
lacked abroad, and it brought into full and
effectual exercise the diplomatic side of the
struggle for independence. It was then
that Franklin showed himself another
Washington. "On the great question of
the foreign relations of the United States,"
says Wharton, "it made no matter whether
he was alone or surrounded by unfriendly
colleagues; it was only through him that
negotiations could be carried on with
France, for to him alone could the French
government commit itself with the con-
sciousness that the enormous confidences

reposed in him would be honorably guarded." France, chiefly through the influence of Franklin, had given covert assistance to the colonies from the beginning of the struggle, but the French ministry hesitated to take a decisive step. Fear that the Americans would succumb, and leave France to bear the weight of British hostility, and apprehension that England might grant the demands of the colonists and then turn her forces against European foes, deterred the French government from avowed support of the American cause. The news from Saratoga gave assurance that America would prove a steadfast as well as a powerful ally, and that with the aid of the United States the British empire might be dismembered, and France avenged for her losses and humiliations on the American continent. Nor was revenge the only motive which led France to cast her lot with the revolted colonies. England was already stretching forth to establish her power in India, and France felt that with North America and India both subject to the British, the maritime and commercial superiority of England would be a menace to other powers.

France did not act without long and careful premeditation on the part of the French crown and its ministers, for the relations between England and her American colonies had been carefully and acutely considered by the statesmen of Versailles long before the point of open revolt was reached. Even when France concluded to throw her resources into the scale on the side of the United States she did not altogether abandon her cautious attitude. The French government acknowledged the United States as a sovereign and treaty-making power; but while the treaty of commerce of February 6, 1778, was absolute and immediate in its effects, the treaty of alliance of the same date was contingent on war taking place between Great Britain and France.

Upon receiving formal notice of the treaties Lord North immediately recalled the British ambassador from Paris, and George III. stated, in bad English, to Lord North (the king spelled "Pennsylvania" "Pensilvania," and "wharfs" "warfs") that a corps must be drawn from the army in America sufficient to attack the French islands. There was a state of partial war without a declaration of war. The naval forces of England and France came into unauthorized collision, and war was the result.

LAKE ERIE.

Upon the struggle for the control of Lake Erie during the War of 1812 depended whether England should succeed in preventing the western growth of the United States, or be driven forever from the soil which Americans claimed as their own. Master-Commandant Oliver Hazard Perry was but twenty-six years of age when the Navy Department called him from his pleasant home at Newport and sent him to command a navy summoned from the primeval forests of the Northwest. Young as he was Perry had seen service in the wars with France and Tripoli, and he had requested the Navy Department at the commencement of the conflict with England to send him where he could meet the enemies of his country. Perry arrived at Erie, then known as Presque Isle, in March, 1813. Sailing-Master Daniel Dobbins and Noah Brown, a shipwright from New York, were busily at work on the new fleet. Two brigs, the Niagara and the Lawrence, were built with white and black oak and chestnut frames, the outside planking being of oak and the decks of pine. Two gunboats were newly planked up, and work on a schooner was just begun. The vessels had to be vigilantly guarded against attack by the British, who were fully aware of the work being done. The capture of Fort George left the Niagara River open, and several American vessels which had been unable before to pass the Canadian batteries were now, with great exertion, drawn into the lake. These were the brig Caledonia, the schooners Somers, Tigress and Ohio, and the sloop Trippe. An English squadron set out to intercept the new arrivals, but Perry succeeded in gaining the harbor of Erie before the enemy made their appearance.

The American ships were ready for sea on July 10, but officers and sailors were lacking, and it was not until about the close of the month that Perry had three hundred men to man his ten vessels. While the British squadron, under Captain Robert Heriot Barclay maintained a vigorous blockade, Perry found that his new brigs could not cross the bar without landing their guns and being blocked up on scows. Commander Barclay, thinking that Perry could not move, made a visit of ceremony with his squadron to Port Dover, on the Canadian side. During Barclay's absence Perry got the Lawrence and Niagara over the bar, and the British commander was astonished when he returned on the morning of August 5, to see the American fleet riding at anchor, and ready for battle. Barclay wished to delay the naval combat until after the completion at Malden of a ten-gun ship called the Detroit, which was to be added to his force, and he therefore put into that harbor.* Perry improved the

---
* Malden, on the Detroit River, eighteen miles below the city of Detroit, is now known as Amherstburg.

delay to exercise his crews, largely made up of soldiers, in seamanship.

It was not until September 10 that the British squadron came out to give battle. Master-Commandant Perry had nine vessels mounting fifty-four guns, with 1536 pounds of metal. The British squadron consisted of six vessels, mounting sixty-three guns, with a total weight of 852 pounds. The American vessels were manned by 400 men and the British by 502 men and boys. In discipline, training and physical condition, however, the difference of crews was much more in favor of the British than the numbers indicate. The brig Lawrence was Perry's flagship; Barclay's pennant flew on the Detroit. As the American vessels stood out to sea Perry hoisted a large blue flag with the words of the dying Lawrence in white muslin—"Don't give up the ship!" He prepared for defeat as well as for victory, by gathering all his important papers in a package weighted and ready to be thrown overboard in the event of disaster. It may be said that Perry fought the earlier part of the battle almost alone, a slow-sailing brig, the Caledonia, being in line ahead of the Niagara, and Perry, having given orders that the vessels should preserve their stations.

In the duel of long guns the British had a decided advantage and their fire being con-

centrated on the Lawrence that vessel soon
became a wreck. Of one hundred and
three men fit for duty on board the American flagship, eighty-three were killed or
wounded. These figures sufficiently indicate the carnage; but Perry fought on.
"Can any of the wounded pull a rope?"
cried Perry, and mangled men crawled out
to help in training the guns. For nearly
three hours the Lawrence with the schooners
Ariel and Scorpion fought the British fleet.
Then Master-Commandant Elliott, of the
Niagara, fearing Perry had been killed,
undertook, notwithstanding Perry's previous orders, to go out of line to the help of
the Lawrence. Perry then changed his flag
to the Niagara, leaving orders with First
Lieutenant John J. Yarnall, of the Lawrence, to hold out to the last. Perry at
once sent Master-Commandant Elliott in a
boat to bring up the schooners, and meantime Lieutenant Yarnall, deciding that further resistance would mean the destruction
of all on board, lowered the flag of the
Lawrence. The English thought they were
already victors, and gave three cheers, but
the Lawrence drifted out of range before
they could take possession of her, and the
Stars and Stripes were raised again over
her blood-stained decks.

The battle had in truth only begun, but
was soon to end. The remainder of the

American squadron closed in on the English vessels, raking them fore and aft. The English officers and men were swept from their decks by the hurricane of iron. It was the United States and the Macedonian on a smaller scale. The American cannonade at close quarters was so fast and furious that the British ships were soon in a condition that left no choice save between sinking or surrender. In fifteen minutes after the Americans closed in a British officer waved a white handkerchief. The enemy had struck. Two of the English vessels, the Chippewa and the Little Belt, sought to escape to Malden, but were pursued and captured by the sloop Trippe and the Scorpion.* Perry proceeded to the Lawrence, and on the decks of his flagship, still slippery with blood, he received the surrender of the English officers. Perry wrote with a pencil on the back of an old

---

* "At half-past two, the wind springing up, Captain Elliott was enabled to bring his vessel, the Niagara, into close action I immediately went on board of her, when he anticipated my wish by volunteering to bring the schooners, which had been kept astern by the lightness of the wind, into close action. At forty-five minutes past two the signal was made for close action. The Niagara being very little injured I determined to pass through the enemy's line, bore up and passed ahead of their two ships and a brig, large schooner and sloop from the larboard side, at half pistol shot distance. The smaller vessels at this time having gotten within grape and canister distance, under the direction of Captain Elliott, and keeping up a well-directed fire, the two ships, a brig and a schooner, surrendered, a schooner and a sloop making a vain attempt to escape."—*Perry's account of the battle.*

letter his famous dispatch: "We have met the enemy, and they are ours—two ships, two brigs, one schooner and one sloop." The Americans lost in the battle twenty-seven killed and ninety-six wounded, of whom twenty-two were killed and sixty-one wounded on board the Lawrence. Twelve of the American quarter-deck officers were killed. The British lost forty-one killed and ninety-four wounded, making a total of one hundred and thirty-five. Commander Barclay, one of Nelson's veterans, had lost an arm in a previous naval engagement. He gave his men an admirable example of courage, being twice wounded, once in the thigh and once in the shoulder, thus being deprived of the use of his remaining arm. Captain Finnis, of the Queen Charlotte, was mortally wounded, and died on the same evening.

Thousands on the American and British shores witnessed or listened to the conflict, conscious that upon the result depended the future of the Northwest. None listened with more patriotic eagerness than John Kinzie, already mentioned as the first resident of Chicago, then a prisoner at Malden, having been removed from Detroit on suspicion that he was in correspondence with General Harrison. Kinzie was taking a promenade under guard, when he heard the guns on Lake Erie. The time allotted to the prisoner for his daily walk expired, but neither he nor his guard observed the fact, so anxiously were they catching every sound from what they now felt sure was an engagement between ships of war. At length Mr. Kinzie was reminded that the hour for his return to confinement had arrived. He pleaded for another half hour.

"Let me stay," said he, "till we can learn how the battle has gone."

Very soon a sloop appeared under press of sail, rounding the point, and presently two vessels in chase of her.

"She is running—she bears the British colors," cried Kinzie—"yes, yes, they are lowering—they are striking her flag! Now" —turning to the soldiers, "I will go back to prison contented. I know how the battle has gone."

The sloop was the Little Belt, the last of the British fleet to surrender, after a vain attempt to escape. The Father of Chicago had seen the end of the battle which made possible the Chicago of to-day.

Perry's victory compelled the enemy to evacuate Detroit, and all their posts in American territory except Michilimacinac, which place remained in the possession of the British until the close of the war. Soon after the battle of Lake Erie, General Harrison crossed to the Canadian shore, entered Malden, and then passed on in pursuit of

Proctor and Tecumseh, who were in full retreat up the valley of the Thames. In the battle of the Thames, which followed, the British were completely routed, and Tecumseh was slain. The Northwest was now secure. The British had been driven back and their Indian ally, Tecumseh, with his great scheme of an independent Indian power, had passed away.

CERRO GORDO.

While the annexation of Texas was the immediate provocation of war between the United States and Mexico, yet the question whether North America should be dominated by men of the British or the Spanish-American race was, like slavery, to be settled only on the battlefield. Up to that decision Mexico believed herself to be in power and prowess, as she was almost in territory, the equal of the United States. The armies of Scott and Taylor proved in some of the best-fought battles of history that the North American Republic was the leading power of the continent.

The American Government and people were not unprepared for a challenge from Mexico, and rather welcomed it, as, apart from the Texas issue, Mexico had, from the time of her independence, treated the United States in a manner far from neigh-

borly, and inflicted many injuries on
American citizens. In the West and South
especially it was deemed necessary to give
Mexico a lesson; in New England the war
was not popular. Hostilities began, and
two sharp battles were fought, before war
was actually declared. General Zachary
Taylor, with a force much inferior to that
of the enemy, defeated the Mexicans at
Palo Alto and Resaca de la Palma, and
drove them out of Texas. At Resaca the
American dragoons under Captain May
charged straight upon a Mexican battery,
killing the gunners and capturing the Mexican general La Vega just as he was about
to apply a match to one of the pieces. The
Mexican army was so completely scattered
that their commander Arista fled unaccompanied across the Rio Grande. At Buena
Vista Generals Taylor and Wool, with 5000
men, of whom only 500 were regular troops,
confronted Santa Anna with 20,000, February 23, 1847. The Mexican chieftain
expected an easy victory, and his army, inspired with his confidence, rushed from
their mountains upon the small force of
Americans drawn up in battle array on the
plain of Angostura.

> "Like the fierce Northern hurricane
> That sweeps his great plateau,
> Flushed with the triumph yet to gain,
> Came down the serried foe.

> Who heard the thunder of the fray
> Break o'er the field beneath,
> Well knew the watchword of that day
> Was victory or death."

The battle lasted all day, the American artillery being splendidly handled, and mowing down the Mexicans at every charge. "Give 'em a little more grape, Captain Bragg!" said Taylor, quietly, as he saw Santa Anna's lines wavering. The grape was given, and the Mexicans fled, leaving 500 of their number dead or dying on the field. The total Mexican loss, including wounded and prisoners was about 2000; that of the Americans in killed, wounded and missing, 746. This victory and the success of Fremont and Kearney in California, completed the conquest of Northern Mexico.

General Winfield Scott, who was in supreme command of all the American forces, conducted a brilliant campaign from the coast. After taking Vera Cruz and the castle of San Juan de Ulloa, General Scott advanced toward the City of Mexico with about 10,000 men. At Cerro Gordo, a difficult pass in the mountains, the American army encountered 12,000 Mexicans under command of Santa Anna, who had, by extraordinary efforts, collected this force after his defeat at Buena Vista. The battle was fought on April 18, every movement of the American troops being directed, according to a carefully prepared plan, by General Scott. Colonel Harvey led the storming party into the pass, with a deep river on one side, and batteries belching death from lofty rocks on the other side. The Americans rushed forward with irresistible courage. They knew their enemy. The Alamo had not been forgotten.

Cerro Gordo fell, and the flight of the Mexicans may best be described in the language of one of their own historians: "General Santa Anna accompanied by some of his adjutants, was passing along the road to the left of the battery, when the enemy's column, now out of the woods, appeared on his line of retreat and fired upon him, forcing him back. The carriage in which he had left Jalapa was riddled with shot, the mules killed and taken by the enemy, as well as a wagon containing $16,000 received the day before for the pay of the soldiers. Every tie of command and obedience now being broken among our troops, safety alone being the object, and all being involved in a frightful confusion, they rushed desperately to the narrow pass of the defile that descended to the Plan del Rio, where the general-in-chief had proceeded, with the chiefs and officers accompanying him. Horrid indeed was the descent by that narrow and rocky path where thousands rushed, disputing the passage with desperation, and leaving a track of blood upon the road. All classes being confounded military distinction and respect were lost; and badges of rank became marks of sarcasm. The enemy, now masters of our camp, turned their guns upon the fugitives, thus augmenting the terror of the multitude that crowded through the defile and pressed forward every instant by a new impulse, which increased the confusion and disgrace of that ill-fated day." Of the 12,000 Mexicans engaged in this battle about 1200 were killed and wounded, and 3000 were made prisoners. The captives were all paroled, and the sick and wounded sent to Jalapa, where they were well cared for. The Castle of Perote, the strongest fortress in Mexico, surrendered without resistance, and the American flag was unfurled on the summit of the eastern Cordilleras.

Cerro Gordo was the decisive engagement, but more fierce conflicts occurred before General Scott planted the American flag, on September 14, 1847, in the City of Mexico. From the National Palace of that Republic General Scott issued a general order in which, with justifiable pride, he declared: "Beginning with August 10 and ending the fourteenth instant, this army has gallantly fought its way through the fields and forts of Contreras, San Antonio,

Churubusco, Molino del Rey, Chapultepec and the gates of San Cosme and Tacubaya into the capital of Mexico. When the very limited number who have performed these brilliant deeds shall have become known, the world will be astonished and our own countrymen filled with joy and admiration.'' The triumphs of Scott and Taylor added luster to American arms which time will not efface. They recall the exploits of Cortes and Pizarro, save in the scrupulous honor and humanity which guided every step of the American invasion. No victors were ever more generous in their treatment of the conquered. ''The soldiers of Vera Cruz,'' says a Mexican historian, ''received the honor due to their valor and misfortunes. Not even a look was given them by the enemy's soldiers which could be interpreted into an insult.'' The Duke of Wellington, the conqueror of Napoleon, followed Scott's campaign with deep interest and caused its movements to be marked on a map daily, as information was received. Admiring its triumphs up to the basin of Mexico, Wellington then said: ''Scott is lost. He has been carried away by success. He can't take the city, and he can't fall back on his base.'' Wellington proved to be wrong. He had never met American troops.

The treaty of Guadalupe-Hidalgo, concluded February 2, 1848, established the

Rio Grande as the boundary between the
United States and Mexico, and California
and New Mexico, including what is now
Arizona, were ceded to the United States
for $15,000,000. The United States also
assumed the payment of obligations due by
Mexico to American citizens to the amount
of $3,250,000, and discharged Mexico
from all claims of citizens of the United
States against that Republic. Strict provision was made for the preservation of the
rights of the inhabitants of the ceded territory. The Gadsden Purchase, in 1853—so
called from General James Gadsden, who
conducted the negotiations in behalf of the
United States—added 45,535 square miles
of Mexican territory to the United States,
for which this country paid $10,000,000,
Mexico at the same time relinquishing
claims against the United States for Indian
depredations amounting to from $15,000,-
000 to $30,000,000. The American Re-
public thus received in all, as a consequence
of the Mexican War, 591,398 square miles,
and the Union acquired its present boundaries, exclusive of Alaska.

The Mexican War gave to the United
States the Pacific as well as the Atlantic sea-
board, and completed the western movement
which had begun with the very birth of the
Republic. It made the United States the
great power of the American continent,

seated between the two oceans, with a domain unequaled in natural resources by any other region of the world.

GETTYSBURG.

Gettysburg is universally regarded as the decisive conflict of the Rebellion. In the beginning of the war the North was at a disadvantage. Mr. Lincoln found the little army of the United States scattered and disorganized, the navy sent to distant quarters of the globe, the treasury bankrupt and the public service demoralized.

Floyd and his fellow-conspirators had done their work thoroughly. It did not take long for the people of the North to rally to the defence of the government, and for an army to be formed capable not only of defending the loyal States, but of striking a blow at the Confederacy. With the National credit restored, an abundance of currency provided for national needs, and the public departments cleared of Southern sympathizers, the North entered upon a conflict which could have but one ending should the Northern States remain steadfast.

The weakness of the South, from a military standpoint, was in the fact that men lost could not be replaced.

The North could replenish its depleted

armies; the South could not. With men therefore of the same race and equal in soldierly qualities arrayed against each other, one side within measurable distance of exhaustion and the other with inexhaustible human resources to draw upon, the war became an easy sum in arithmetic, provided the stronger party should not cry "enough" before the weaker had reached the exhaustion point. The battles on comparatively equal terms were fought, therefore, in the early part of the war, the decisive battles in 1863, and the closing struggle between the gasping Confederacy and the Union stronger than ever, in the last fifteen months of the conflict.

While, under the able generalship of Grant and Sherman, the Union forces in the West made steady progress, almost from the beginning of the war, in the East the record of our armies was for nearly two years one of almost monotonous defeat. The tide turned at Gettysburg. General George Gordon Meade succeeded General Joseph Hooker in command of the Army of the Potomac. Meade was not a brilliant man, but he was a thorough soldier, and eminently free from that spirit of envy which was the bane of our armies, which had nearly driven Grant from the service, and which was responsible for the loss of more than one battle. Elated by Chancel-

lorsville, Lee determined to invade the
North. The South made an extreme effort
to replenish its armies, and that of Northern Virginia was raised to about 100,000
men. With the greater part of this magnificent host, including 15,000 cavalry and
280 guns, Lee marched down the Shenandoah Valley, crossed the Potomac on the
twenty-fifth of June, and headed for Chambersburg. Meade drew near with the Army
of the Potomac, and such reinforcements as
had been hastily collected in Pennsylvania
on the news of the invasion.

At Gettysburg the two armies met for the
decisive battle of the war. Meade had on
the field 83,000 men and 300 guns; Lee,
69,000 men and 250 guns. For three days
the two armies contended with frightful
losses, and with a courage not surpassed in
ancient or modern warfare. The brave
General John F. Reynolds lost his life in
the first encounter, and General Winfield
Scott Hancock was sent by Meade to take
charge of the field. On the second day occurred the desperate conflict for Little
Round Top, which resulted in that key to
the Union line being seized and held by
the Union troops. Neither side, however,
gained any decided advantage. On the
third day Lee prepared for the grand movement known in history as "Pickett's
Charge." Fourteen thousand men were

selected as the forlorn hope of the Confederacy. For two hours before the charge 120 guns kept up a fearful cannonade upon the Union lines. Meade answered with eighty guns. About three o'clock in the afternoon Meade ceased firing. Lee thought the Northern gunners were silenced. He was mistaken; they knew what was coming.

On moved the charging column, as the smoke of battle lifted, and the "tattered uniforms and bright muskets" came plainly into view. At an average distance of about eleven hundred yards the Union batteries opened. Shot and shell tore through the Confederate ranks. Still they marched on over wounded and dying and dead. Canister now rained on their ranks, and as they came within closer range a hurricane of bullets burst upon them, and men dropped on every side like leaves in the winds of autumn. The strength of the charging column melted before the gale of death; but the survivors staggered on. When the remains of the Confederate right reached the Union works their three brigade commanders had fallen, every field officer except one had been killed or wounded; but still the remnant kept its face to the foe, led to annihilation by the dauntless Armistead. The four brigades on the left of Pickett met a similar fate. "They moved up splendidly," wrote a Union officer, "deploying as they crossed the long sloping interval. The front of the column was nearly up the slope, and within a few yards of the Second Corps' front and its batteries, when suddenly a terrific fire from every available gun on Cemetery Ridge burst upon them. Their graceful lines underwent an instantaneous transformation in a dense cloud of smoke and dust; arms, heads, blankets, guns and knapsacks were tossed in the air, and the moan from the battlefield was heard amid the storm of battle."

One half of the 14,000 perished in the charge. Gettysburg was over, and the tide of invasion from the South was rolled back never to return. Meade had lost about 23,000 men, and Lee probably many more than this number. His loss was not officially reported. Halleck, whose business as general-in-chief seemed to be to annoy successful commanders, and irritate them to the resignation point, blamed Meade for allowing Lee to retire without another battle, but public opinion upheld the victor of Gettysburg, and Congress honored him and Generals Hancock and O. O. Howard with a resolution of thanks.

The writer has been told by a veteran of Gettysburg that from that eventful Fourth of July a new spirit seemed to animate the

Union troops. They saw that they could defeat the Confederates under the ablest Confederate commander, and the depression of former disasters was lifted from the breasts of our soldiers. Besides they justly looked upon Lee's retreat as a final retreat, and went forward with fresh courage toward the goal which at last appeared within reach. The Confederacy never recovered from Gettysburg.

XVIII.—GREAT RELIGIOUS MOVEMENTS OF THE CENTURY.

BY DR. B. J. FERNIE.

Looking back over the path humanity has traversed through the past centuries, we see that the trend has ever been upward. The new course the world has taken at every turning-point has been into clearer light and into better conditions. The race has not been traveling in a circle, and it has not been obliged to retrace its steps. Every point gained has been the stepping-stone to a new advance. Material and moral progress can be traced from age to age, and the end is not yet. There are heights yet to be scaled and evils yet to be extirpated. Religion and philanthropy, hand in hand, are preparing for a new advance great as those that lie behind us. What has been accomplished in recent times encourages us to hope for even greater triumphs. The energy of exploration, the activity of science, and the progress of invention have had their parallels in new applications of spiritual truth and new organizations for effecting spiritual regeneration. A brief survey of the past century will show not only the progress made, but the character of the forces that are gathered for a new advance.

DEFENCE ON NEW LINES.

In a period so intensely active and progressive as the nineteenth century has been, in politics, science and literature, it would have been surprising if the Church had remained inert, wrapped like a mummy in the cerements of the past. At the beginning of the century, there were voices on all hands loudly proclaiming that it was dead; that it was antiquated and obsolete; that it had lost touch with the life of the time, that it was a relic of exploded superstition; and as a great writer said, had fallen into a godless mechanical condition, standing as the lifeless form of a church, a mere case of theories, like the carcass of a once swift camel, left withering in the thirst of the universal desert. That in certain circles there was ground for such reproach is sufficiently proved. Materialism had crept into its colleges, sapping away their spiritual life and driving young men either into Atheism or into the Roman Catholic Communion. Such activity as it had, was in the evangelical circles only.

The common people still listened eagerly to Wesley's successors and were intensely in earnest in the Christian life and work. It was at the top that the tree was dying, where the currents of the philosophy of Voltaire struck the branches, and where Hume's scorching radicalism blighted its leaves. In the universities, and the clubs, not in the workshops, was religion scorned and contemned.

There was soon, however, to be a quickening of the dry bones. The spirit of the time—the zeit-geist—began to move in the Church. It was the spirit of investigation, of scientific inquiry, of rigorous test. The older preachers and religious authorities still droned about the duty of defending the faith "once for all" delivered to the saints. In spite of their protests, the younger men would go down into the crypt of the Church, and examine the foundations of the building. They could not be kept back by authoritative assurances that the stones were sound, and were well and truly laid. The hysterical protests against the irreverence of examination fell on deaf ears. The answer was the simple insistance on investigation. The very reluctance to permit it was an indication that it would not bear investigation.

At the opening of the century, this idea, expressed in varying forms, was rapidly

becoming prevalent. The citadel of the
Church was assaulted, by some with ferocity,
and by others with scorn and contempt.
The defence was on the old lines
of denunciation of the wickedness of the
assailants, of vituperative epithets, and of
the assumption of special and divine illumination.
The issue of the conflict would not
have been doubtful, had it been continued
with these tactics. The Church would have
been relegated to the limbo of superstition
and the hide-bound pedantry of ecclesiasticism,
if new defenders on new principles
had not entered the lists. Reinforcement
came from a band of philosophic thinkers
of whom Wordsworth and Coleridge were
the pioneers. The influence of both these
men was underestimated at the time. They
appeared weak and ineffective, but the
ideas to which they gave expression, entered
the minds of stronger men, who applied
them with more vigorous force. The
Church, Coleridge declared, as Carlyle interprets
him, was not dead, but tragically
asleep only. It might be aroused and
might again become useful, if only the
right paths were opened. Coleridge could
not open the paths, he could but vaguely
show the depth and volume of the forces
pent up in the Church; but he insisted that
they were there, that eternal truth was in
Christianity, and that out of it must come

the light and life of the world. As his little band of hearers listened to him, they saw the first faint gleams of the light which was to illumine the world and make the darkness and degradation of the materialistic philosophy an impossibility to the devout mind. Thus he stood at the beginning of the nineteenth century, as Erasmus stood at the beginning of the sixteenth, perceiving and proclaiming the existence of truths which others were to apply to the needs of the time.

To ascertain precisely in what form the forces of Christianity existed and how they might be applied to nineteenth century life, became early in the nineteenth century the problem on which the best thought of the time was concentrated. Coleridge's unshaken conviction that it was solvable, inspired many with courage. Whately, Arnold, Schleiermacher, Bunsen, Ewald, Newman, Hare, Milman, Thirlwall and many others, approached it from different directions. The spirit of scientific investigation that was in the air was applied with reverent hands, but with unsparing resolve to ascertain the exact truth. The investigation was no longer confined to dogma; a proof text from the Bible was no longer sufficient to close a controversy. The Bible itself must be subjected to investigation. This was indeed going to the foundations.

There was a wild outcry against rationalism and iconoclasm, but the search for truth and fact went on. As in a siege, the garrison must sometimes destroy with their own hands outworks which cannot be successfully defended, and may be made a vantage ground for the enemy, so the defenders of Christianity set themselves to the task of finding out how much of the current theology was credible and tenable, and how much might wisely be abandoned, to insure the safety of the remainder. The discoveries of Geology, Astronomy and of Biology could not be denied, yet their testimony was contrary to Christian doctrine. "The world was made in six natural days," said the old Christian preacher. "The world was thousands of years in the making," said the geologist. The preacher appealed to his Bible, the geologist appealed to the rocks. The issue was fairly joined, and in the early years of the century it seemed as if there was no alternative but that of believing the Bible and denying science, or believing science and giving up the Bible; it seemed impossible to believe both. When the scientific theologian ventured to suggest that the word "day," might mean age, or period, there was another outcry that the Bible was being surrendered to the enemy. But it was realized that the message of the Bible to the world was not scientific, and that its usefulness was not impaired by the suggested mode of understanding its record of creation; and gradually the surrender was accepted. It is true that to this day there are some who will not accept it, as there is at least one preacher who insists, on the authority of the Bible, that "the sun do move," but the number diminishes in every generation. A beginning was made in attaining the true view of the Bible which led further and has not yet reached its limits. Having admitted that the Bible was not given to teach science the Church has to decide whether it can admit the theory of evolution and whether its records of history are authoritative. These questions are so fundamental that the strife of Calvinism and Arminianism and the question of the double procession of the Holy Spirit, which seemed vital to our fathers have faded into relative insignificance.

Evangelical Activity.

While these storms were agitating the upper air, and the thunderous echoes reverberated through the mountains, the work on the plain went rapidly forward. However the scholars and the theologians might decide the questions at issue between them, the working forces were profoundly convinced that the Gospel was the great need of the world, and they put out new energy and applied all the powers of the mind to devising new methods for its propagation. The increased facilities of travel, the improved means of communication and, above all, the power of the printing-press, were all seized and harnessed to service in the dissemination of the Gospel. No characteristic of this century is so prominent as this intense activity and aggressive energy. From every secular movement, the Church has taken suggestions for its own advancement. Trade-unionism has suggested Christian Endeavor and the Evangelical Alliance; the public school system has developed the International Lesson system in the Sunday School; the political convention has taught the advantages of great religious conferences; the principles of military organization have been utilized in the Salvation Army. If in some circles religion seems to have been a fight over doctrines and theories, in others it has seemed a ceaseless, untiring struggle for converts. In no century since the first century of the Christian era has the zeal of propagation, with no element of proselytism in it, taken so strong a hold of the followers of Christ. To translate the Bible into every tongue, to carry the Gospel message to every people, and to evangelize the masses at home, prodigious efforts have been put forth, and enormous sums of money have been expended. Mental activity, uncompromising veracity, indefatigable energy, have characterized the Church through the century, and its closing years show no abatement in any of these characteristics. A brief sketch of some of the more prominent of these developments can render the fact only more obvious.

BIBLE REVISION.

One of the most important events of the century to the English speaking world is the Revision of the Bible. Its full effect is not yet felt, as the book which was the product of the Revisers' labors is but slowly winning its way into use in the Church and the home. Like its predecessor, the Authorized Version now in general use, it has to encounter the prejudice which comes from long familiarity with the book in use and from the veneration for the phraseology in which the precious truths are expressed. Yet from the beginning of the century the need of an improved translation was felt and several persons undertook to supply it, but with very objectionable results. The principal bases of the need were serious. One was that many words and phrases have in the nineteenth century a meaning entirely different from the one they had in the early part of the seventeenth century when the Authorized Version was issued. One case in point is Mark vi. 25, in which Salome asks that the head of John the Baptist be given her "by and by in a charger." In 1611 the expression by and by meant immediately or forthwith, and was a correct translation, while with us it means a somewhat indefinite future and is therefore an incorrect translation. With the noun, too, the meaning has changed. Our idea of a charger is of a war-horse, not of a dish, which the original conveys. A second reason for the revision was that there were in the libraries in this century several manuscripts of the original, much older than those to which the translators of the Authorized Version had access when they undertook their work. A third reason was that a notable advance had been made in scholarship in the interval, and learned men were much better acquainted with the Hebrew and Greek idiom than were any of the scholars of the King James period. For these three, among other reasons, a revision was necessary, that the unlearned reader might have, as nearly as was possible, the exact equivalent in English of the words of the Bible writers. The project, after being widely discussed for several years, finally took shape in England in 1870, when the Convocation of Canterbury appointed two

committees to undertake the work. The
ablest scholars in Hebrew and Greek literature in the country were assigned to the
committees, of which one was engaged on
the Old, and the other on the New Testament.
They were empowered to call to their aid
similar committees in America, who might
work simultaneously with them. Stringent
instructions were given to them to avoid
making changes where they were not clearly
needed for the accuracy of translation, and
to preserve the idiom of the Authorized
Version. Only with these safeguards and
with not a little reluctance, the commission
was issued. One hundred and one scholars
on both sides of the Atlantic took part in
the work. The committees commenced
their labors early in 1871. On May 17,
1881, the Revised New Testament was
issued, and on May 21, 1885, the Revised
Old Testament was in the hands of the
public. All that scholarship, strenuous
labor and exhaustive research could do to
give a faithful translation had been done
within the somewhat narrow and conservative limits under which the revisers were
commissioned.

BIBLES BY THE MILLION.

With this improvement, there was at the
same time a marked impetus in Bible circulation. The nineteenth century has been

eminently a Bible-reading and a Bible-studying period. In no previous century have efforts on so gigantic a scale been made to put the Book in the hands of every one who could read it. The price was brought so low by the decrease in the cost of production, that the very poorest could possess a copy. The British and Foreign Bible Society, founded in 1804, and the American Bible Society, founded in 1816, have largely contributed to this result. Both societies were organized to issue the Bible without note or comment, and both have faithfully labored to promote its circulation. In spite of all that has been said against the Book and in spite of the fact that so large a number of persons must have been supplied, the circulation has increased from year to year. In the year ending March, 1896, the American Society alone issued 1,750,000 copies, and the British two and a half million. During its existence the American Society has sent out over sixty-one million copies and the British Society over one hundred and forty millions. The work of translation has kept pace with the demand. At the beginning of the century the Bible had been translated, in whole or in part, into thirty-eight languages. It is now translated into three hundred and eighty-one, and translators are engaged on nearly a hundred others. Nor must it be supposed that the supply was in excess of the demand. There is abundant evidence of the desire of the public to possess the Word of God. One fact alone is a conspicuous proof of this demand. In 1892 the proprietor of the *Christian Herald* of New York offered an Oxford Teacher's Bible as a premium with his journal. The offer was accepted with such avidity that edition after edition was exhausted, and it has been renewed every year since with increased demand. Through this journal alone, by this means, over three hundred and two thousand copies have been put into the hands of the people during the past five years.

With the increase in the circulation of the Word of God there has been a costly and thorough effort to gain new light on its pages. Never before have labor and money been expended so lavishly in endeavors to learn from exploration and research, historical facts which would contribute to an intelligent understanding of its history and literature. In 1865 a society called the Palestine Exploration Society was organized for the special purpose of thoroughly examining the Holy Land, investigating and identifying ancient sites and making exact maps of the country. In twenty-seven years the society, though working with the utmost economy, expended

$425,000. The result of its labors has been to let a flood of light on the ancient places and the ancient customs of its people, explaining many allusions in the sacred history, poetry and prophecy that were previously dark. The Egypt Exploration Fund has also added materially to our knowledge of that country which is associated with the early history of the Chosen People. But the most valuable aid to Bible study came from the discovery of the Assyrian Royal Library, a series of clay tablets and cylinders covered with cuneiform inscriptions which were deciphered by Mr. George Smith of the British Museum. From these and from the records on the monuments of Egypt historical information has been derived of inestimable value in the study of the Bible.

A Great Missionary Era.

One of the most prominent characteristics of the Church of Christ in this century has been its phenomenal missionary activity. Its zeal in this cause, the devotion and courage of its missionaries and the amount of money expended have had no parallel in the previous history of the Church. Already a beginning had been made when the century dawned. In 1701 King William III. of England had granted a charter to the Society for the Propagation of the

Gospel in Foreign Parts. In 1714 Frederick IV. of Denmark established a College of Missions and two Danish missionaries were laboring in India. In 1721 the famous Danish missionary, Hans Egede, began a work in Greenland. In 1732 the Moravian missionaries, Dober and Nitschmann, went to St. Thomas, and in the following year the Moravian Church sent missionaries to Labrador, the West Indies, South America, South Africa and India. But it was not until the last decade of the eighteenth century that the spirit which was to distinguish the next century really manifested itself. In 1792 the devotion and consecration of William Carey led to the formation of the Baptist Missionary Society, and in the following year he sailed for India as its first missionary.

In 1795 the London Missionary Society was organized, a missionary ship was purchased and the first band of missionaries sailed for the South Sea Islands. Two years later, another party sailed for South Africa, among whom were the veterans, Vanderkemp and Kitchener. Two Scottish societies were founded in 1796 and a Dutch Society in 1797. In the closing year of the century the famous Church Missionary Society was formed in the Church of England. Thus the nineteenth century opened with organizations for work in existence and pioneers, few in number but intensely in earnest in several fields of labor.

The first quarter of the century witnessed the advent of new agencies, as well as a multiplication of forces. The American Board of Commissioners for Foreign Missions was organized in 1810, the English Wesleyan Missionary Society in 1814, the American Baptist in 1814, the American Methodist in 1819, the American Protestant Episcopal in 1820, and the Berlin and Paris Missionary Societies in 1824. Thus, in the comparatively short space of thirty-two years, thirteen societies had been organized by the various denominations here and in Europe, each of which was destined to grow to proportions little contemplated by their founders. Since that time the great China Inland Mission and other undenominational societies have been founded and are sending out men and women in large numbers to the heathen world. Besides these, there have been societies of special workers which have done valuable service in aiding the missionary societies, such as the medical missionaries, the Zenana Missionaries and the university and students' volunteer movements. Statistics recently compiled show that the number of central stations in heathen lands occupied by Protestant missionaries in 1896 was 5055, with out-stations to the number of 17,813. There are now thirty-seven missionary societies in this country alone which have sent out 3512 missionaries. A library of volumes would be needed to give even a sketch of the results of the labors of these devoted men and women. The Church holds their names in holy reverence. Many of them have attained the crown of martyrdom, and a still greater number have fallen victims to the severities of uncongenial climates. Every heathen land has now associated with it the name of valiant soldiers of the Cross, who have given their lives to add it to their Master's kingdom. In India among many others there have been Carey, Duff, Martyn, Marshman and Ward. In China, Morrison, Milne, Taylor, John Talmage and Griffith John. In Africa, Moffat, Livingstone, Hannington and Vanderkemp. In the South Seas, Williams, Logan and Paton, while Judson of Burmah and a host of noble men and women in every clime, have toiled and suffered, not counting their lives dear unto them, that they might preach to the heathen the unsearchable riches of Christ.

PREACHING TO HEATHEN AT HOME.

The zeal for the propagation of the Gospel among the heathen, has been paralleled by the efforts put forth for the evangelization of the people in nominally Christian lands. In this enterprise the front rank on both sides of the Atlantic has been occupied by the Methodist Church. Its system of itinerary, relieving its ministers in part from exhausting study, and so giving them time and opportunity for pastoral work and aggressive evangelistic effort, its welcome of lay assistance in pulpit service and its system of drill and inspection in the class-meeting, have all combined to develop its working resources and increase its aggressive power. The fact that there are now in the world over thirty million Methodists of various kinds, makes it difficult to realize that when the century began, John Wesley had been dead only nine years. This century consequently has witnessed the growth and development of that mighty organization from the seed sown by that one consecrated man and his helpers. It is doubtful whether in politics or society there is any fact of the century so remarkable as this. The Church Wesley founded has split into sections in this land and in England, but the divisions are one at heart, and the name of Methodist is the common precious possession of them all. A great writer has contended with much force that the world at this day knows no such unifier of nationalities and societies as the Methodist Church. When the young man leaves the parental roof of a Methodist family for some distant city, or some foreign land, the pangs of anxiety are alleviated by the knowledge that wherever he may be, there will be some Methodist Church where he will find friends, and some Methodist classleader who will look after his most important interests. The magnificent Methodist organization, unequalled outside the Roman Catholic Church, has developed within the century, and its aggressive forces have been felt throughout Christendom. All the denominations have received an impetus from its abundant energy and each in its measure has caught the contagion of its activities. In country districts, in the great cities and in foreign lands, its representatives, loyal to their Church and the principles of its founder, are pressing forward in self-denial and apostolic fervor foremost everywhere in the van of the Christian army.

Kindred with the Methodist in its enthusiasm and still more highly organized, is the youngest of all the religious organizations — the Salvation Army. In its origin, a daughter of the Methodist Church, with a strong resemblance in spirit and purpose and methods to its mother, the Salvation Army has a mission peculiarly its own. It too has grown with a rapidity unexampled in the religious history of other centuries. More than one quarter of the century had passed when William Booth first saw the light, more than half the

century had passed before he had begun to
give his life to his Master's service. From
1857 to 1859 he was simply a Methodist
minister, at an unimportant town, appointed
by his conference, poorly paid, and certain
to be removed to another sphere at the end of
his term. In 1865, he and his devoted wife
resigned home and income and dependence
on conference for support, and went to
London. They settled in the poorest and
most degraded district of the city, and
began to preach in tents, in cellars, in deserted saloons, under railroad arches, in
factories and in any place which could be
had for nothing, or at a low rental. The
people gathered in multitudes wherever Mr.
Booth and his wife preached, veritable
heathen, many of them, who knew nothing
of the Bible and had never attended a religious service in their lives. Converts were
numerous and they were required to testify
to the change in their souls and their lives
and to become missionaries in their turn.
In 1870 an old market was purchased in
the densest centre of poverty in London
and was made the headquarters of the Mission. Bands of men and women were sent
out to hold meetings, sing hymns and "give
their testimony" in the open-air, in saloons,
or any resort where an audience could be
gathered. These bands were busy every
night in a hundred wretched districts of

the great city, and at every stand, some poor forlorn creatures would be gathered in and encouraged to begin a new life of faith in Christ. Some method of organization became necessary, and was eventually devised. The perfect obedience and confidence manifested everywhere to the man who directed the movement, and the entire dependence of every worker on him for guidance and support, may have suggested the military system. However that may be, the military organization was adopted, and a perfect system framed with the aid of Railton, Smith, and a few other clever organizers who were attracted to Mr. Booth's side by the novelty of his methods, and his marvelous success. In the spring of 1878, the plans were all matured and the new movement became a compact and powerful religious force. Since that time it has spread throughout England, into several European lands, to the United States, and Canada, to India, Australia and South Africa. Its autocratic character has been steadfastly maintained. General Booth has retained absolute control of every officer in his service and has the management of the enormous income of the army. Occasionally there has been mutiny which has been overcome by tact or prompt discipline, and not until this year (1896), when General Booth's son, Ballington, who was his representative in the United States, resigned rather than be removed from his command, has there been any formidable defiance of the supreme and despotic government of the world-wide organization. The methods of the Army are unconventional and are shocking to staid, respectable members of churches, but criticism is out of place in any method which will redeem the masses in the numbers won by the Salvation Army.

Churches Drawing Together.

A notable characteristic of the religious life of the century, especially in the latter half of it, has been a desire manifested in various quarters, and in different ways, for union among the denominations. That organic union could be attained, no practical man could hope. Uniformity could not be expected, even if it could be proved to be desirable, but friendly association was possible, and there were many who contended that there ought to be a recognition of brotherhood and comradeship, which might issue in some attempt at co-operation. This was the conviction of many prominent preachers and laymen on both sides of the Atlantic, early in the century. And truly the condition of the world and of society was of a character to force such a conviction on the minds of intelligent men. Infidelity was rampant, and intemperance, gambling, unchastity, and other forms of vice were practiced with unblushing effrontery. On the other side, the churches, which should have been waging war on all ungodliness, were fighting each other, contending about the questions on which they differed, and exhausting their strength in internecine conflict. Was it not time, men were asking, that the forces that were on the side of godliness united in opposition to evil? After long discussion, and some opposition, this feeling took practical shape in the Evangelical Alliance. At a meeting held in London in 1846 eight hundred representatives of fifty denominations were assembled. It was found that however widely they differed on questions of doctrine and church government, there was practical agreement on a large number of vital subjects, such as the need of religious education, the observance of the Lord's Day, and the evil influence of infidelity. An organization was effected, on the principles of federation, to secure united action on subjects on which all were agreed, and this organization has been maintained to the present time. Branches have been formed in twenty-seven different lands, each dealing with matters peculiarly affecting the community in which it operates, and by correspondence, and periodical international conferences, keeping in touch with each other. Its usefulness has been proved in the success of its efforts to secure tolerance in several lands, where men were being persecuted for conscience' sake, though much still remains to be done on this line. Perhaps the most conspicuous result of its work is the general observance throughout Christendom of the first complete week of every year as a week of prayer. The proposal for such an observance was made in 1858. Since that time the Alliance has issued every year a list of subjects which are common objects of desire to all Evangelical Christians. On each day of the week, prayer is now offered in every land for the special blessing which is suggested as the topic for the day.

From the same spirit of Christian brotherhood which took shape in the Evangelical Alliance, came at later dates other movements which are yet in their infancy. One of these is the Reunion Conference which meets annually at Grindelwald in Switzerland. Its object is to find a basis for organic union of the Protestant Episcopal Church with Congregationalists, Presbyterians, Methodists and other evangelical denominations. The meetings have been hitherto remarkably harmonious, and suggestions of mutual concessions have been made which have been favorably considered. A less ambitious, and therefore more hopeful movement of like spirit, is that of the Municipal or Civic Church. Its aim is the organization of a federative council of the churches of a city, or of sections of a city, for united effort in social reform, benevolent enterprise and Christian government. It proposes to substitute local co-operation for the existing union on denominational lines, or to add the one to the other. It would unite the Methodist, Baptist, Congregational and other churches in a city, or district, in a movement to restrict the increase of saloons, to insist on the enforcement of laws against immorality and to promote the moral and spiritual welfare of the community. The united voice of the Christians of a city uttered by a council, in which all are represented, would unquestionably exercise an influence more potent than is now exerted by separate action. To these movements must be added another which has been launched under the name of the Brotherhood of Christian Unity. This is a fraternity of members of churches and members of no church, who yet accept Christ as their leader and obey the two cardinal precepts of Christianity—love to God and love to man. Its object is to promote brotherly feeling among Christians and a sense of comradeship among men of different creeds. All these movements are an indication of the spirit of the time. As one of the leaders has said, their aim is not so much to remove the fences which divide the denominations, as to lower them sufficiently to enable those who are within them to shake hands over them. In no previous century since the disintegrating tendency began to manifest itself, has this spirit of brotherly recognition of essential unity been so general, or has taken a shape so hopeful of practical beneficence.

ORGANIZED ACTIVITIES.

Effective influence to the same end has been set in motion, incidentally, by an organization which was originated for a different purpose. This is the Christian Endeavor Society, which is one of the latest of the important religious movements of the century. It was primarily designed to promote spiritual development among young people. It had its birth in 1881 in a Congregational Church at Portland, Me. Dr. Francis E. Clark, the pastor of the church, had a number of young people around him who had recently made public profession of faith in Christ and pledged themselves to His service. Precisely what that implied, may not have been definitely understood by any of them. As every pastor is aware, the period immediately following such a profession is a critical time in the life of every young convert. In the college or the office, or the store, the youth comes in contact with people who have made no profession of the kind, and he is apt to ask himself, and to be asked, in what way he differs from them. The early enthusiasm of his new relation to the Church is liable to decline, and he may become doubtful whether any radical change has taken place in him. He does not realize that he is at the beginning of a period of growth, a gradual process, which is to be lifelong. Taking his conception of personal religion from the sermons he has heard and the appeals that have been made to him, he has a tendency to regard conversion as an experience complete and final, an occult mysterious transformation, effected in a moment and concluded. Disappointment is inevitable, and when non-Christian influences are strong, there is a probability of his drifting into indifference. Dr. Clark was aware of this fact, as other pastors were, by sad experience, and he sought means to remedy it. Some plan was needed which would help the young convert and teach him how to apply his religion to his daily life, to make it an active influence, instead of a past experience. The plan Dr. Clark adopted was of an association of young people in his Church, who should meet weekly for prayer and mutual encouragement and helpfulness, with so much of an aggressive quality as to exert an influence over young people outside its membership. The plan succeeded. The religious force in the soul, so liable to become latent, became active, and the young converts made rapid progress. Dr. Clark explained his experiment to other pastors, who tried it with like results. The remedy for a widespread defect was found. It was adopted on all hands and by all evangelical denominations. It spread from church to church, from town to town and into foreign lands. Annual conventions of these Christian Endeavor Societies were held, at which forty or fifty thousand young people, representing societies in all sections of the country with an aggregate membership of about two million souls, were present to recount their experience and pledge themselves anew to the service. The basis of their association was made so broad that Christians of every denomination could heartily unite in its profession of faith. Thus, in addition to the primary design, a basis of Christian inter-denominational union was incidentally discovered, and the Methodist and the Presbyterian, the Congregationalist and Episcopalian found themselves united in a common bond for a common purpose. The movement in these present years shows no signs of decrease, but is still growing in numbers, power and influence, and promises to be one of the most potent factors of religious life which springing up in this century will go on to influence the next.

The idea of association and combination in religious life, of which Christian Endeavor is the most extensive illustration, has been embodied during the century in other forms. Springing directly from the Christian Endeavor Society, are the Epworth League in the Methodist Church, and the Baptist Young People's Union in the Baptist communion. The two organizations are practically identical in principle and purpose with the Christian Endeavor Society and differ from it only in the absence of the inter-denominational character. The heads of the Methodist Church apprehended danger to their young people in their being members of a society not under direct Methodist control and feared that they might eventually be lost to Methodism. The Baptists, on the other hand, were not concerned on the question of control, but feared that the association of their young people with the young people of other churches might lead them to think lightly of the peculiar rite which separates them from other denominations, and to diminish its importance in their esteem. Both denominations therefore organized societies of the same kind, to keep their young people within the denominational fold.

Another organization which has attained large membership and has become international, is that of the King's Daughters. As its name indicates, it was primarily intended for women, though as it extended, it added as an adjunct a membership for men as King's Sons. It also was interdenominational in character, and its objects were more directly identified with the philanthropic side of the religious life than were those of the societies previously mentioned. It originated in a meeting of ten ladies, held in New York, in 1886, at which plans were discussed for aiding the poor, the unfortunate and the distressed in mind, body or soul. They were all Christian ladies who recognized the duty of ministering in Christ's name to those who were in need and so fulfilling His injunction of kindly service. The plan finally adopted was to organize circles of ten members each, who should be pledged to use their opportunities, as far as they were able, for Christian ministration. Each member agreed to wear, as a badge of the Order, a small silver Maltese Cross, bearing the initials, I. H. N., representing the motto, "In His Name." Every circle was to be left free to apply the principle of service as it saw fit, or as special circumstances might suggest, and all the circles to be under the direction and limited control of a central council. The plan, subsequently modified as experience suggested, was widely adopted. The circles have worked in a variety of ways, visiting hospitals and prisons, making garments for the poor, raising funds for the needy, aiding the churches and rendering service in various ways in which kindly Christian women are so effective.

Still another form of combination in Christian work has distinguished this century. In 1844 George Williams, a London dry-goods merchant employing a large number of young men, made an effort to provide them with a species of Christian club. His own experience as a young man fresh from a country home, suddenly inducted into the temptations of city life, suggested to him the kind of help such young men needed. A Christian friend in a great city to help a new-comer, to find him wholesome amusement in the evenings, and to put him on his guard against the pitfalls that were set for his unwary feet, might, Mr. Williams was convinced, save many a young man from ruin. To provide them with such friends and to furnish a place of meeting for reading, converse and amusement, was the problem the kindly Christian man attempted to solve. Out of his effort grew the institution we know as the Young Men's Christian Association. which has its mission in nearly every large town in this country and in England. The young man of this century can go into no considerable town without finding a commodious hall, with well-equipped library and reading-room, generally with a gymnasium attached, and with a host of young men ready to make his acquaintance and surround him with Christian influences. In many towns, the institution has developed from the purely religious enterprise into a many-sided effort to give practical educational training and to attract young men to it by the help it renders them in secular pursuits. The institution as it now exists, must be counted as one of the most beneficent in its far-reaching influence that the century has produced.

HUMANITARIAN WORK.

Kindred in spirit, but differing essentially in operation, is the institution, peculiarly a product of nineteenth century religion, which we know as the Social or College Settlement. Though it does not claim a distinctively religious character, its principles are so thoroughly identical with Christianity, that no survey of the religious life of the century would be complete without a recognition of it. It is the spirit that brought the Founder of Christianity to the earth, to live a lowly life among men, which inspires the Social Settlement. It is generally an unostentatious house in some crowded neighborhood, where the people are poor and life is hard. In the house are a number of college-bred men, or women, who come in relays and live there for a week or a month or longer. They do no missionary work, do not preach, or denounce, or instruct their neighbors, but they live among them a cleanly, helpful, friendly life, welcoming them cordially as visitors, advising them if advice is sought, rendering help in difficulties and being neighborly in the best sense of the word. There are concerts in the house, exhibitions of pictures, children's parties and amusements of various kinds to which all the neighbors are welcome. Charity is no part of the Settlement's programme. It does not give, but it extends a brotherly hand, and in a spirit of friendship and equality seeks to do a brother's part in brightening lowly lives. Hundreds of such institutions are in operation on both sides the Atlantic. To the credit of this century be it said that it has seen in these institutions the Parable of the Good Samaritan made a living fact in intelligent organization.

Tending directly toward the same object, is the religious enterprise now commonly known as the Institutional Church. It is a distinct gain to the Church if the people in its vicinity discover that it is anxious to help them to a better and happier life in this world, as well as guiding them to happiness in the next. The Divine Founder of Christianity never ignored the fact that men have bodies which need saving, as well as souls, and some of His followers are following His example. Their churches do not stand closed and silent from Sunday to Sunday, but are open every day and evening, busy with some form of practical helpfulness. Temperance societies, coal clubs, sewing meetings, dime savings banks, gymnasiums, boys' clubs, and a host of helpful associations tending to the betterment of life, find their home under the roof of the church, and the pastor and his helpers are finding out the social and economical needs of the people by actual contact with them and devising means to supply them. The critics say this is not the business of the Church, but they are not found among the people who derive benefit from this form of thoughtful interest in their welfare.

THE SUNDAY SCHOOL.

Of all the products of this prolific nineteenth century, the one most extensive and most profitable to the Church still remains to be mentioned. Though this century did not see the birth of the Sunday School, it has witnessed its wonderful development. In June, 1784, Robert Raikes published his famous letter outlining his plan for the religious instruction of children on the Lord's Day, and before the close of the year, John Wesley wrote that he found Sunday Schools springing up wherever he went, and added with prophetic insight: "Perhaps God may have a deeper end therein than men are aware of. Who knows but some of these schools may become nurseries for Christians?" Within five years, a quarter of a million children were gathered into the Sunday Schools. So much had already been done before the beginning of the century. But even then men did not realize whereunto the movement was destined to grow. Probably no enterprise has really exerted a deeper and stronger influence on the religious life of the time. Children have entered the schools, passed through their grades, have become teachers in their turn, and their descendants have followed in their footsteps, until now we can scarcely bring ourselves to believe that a little more than a hundred years ago the Sunday School was unknown. The organization of Sunday School Unions, the introduction of the International Lesson System, and the City, State and National Conventions are all the developments of this century. The thought that a million and a half of Sunday School teachers are now engaged in every clime, Sunday by Sunday, in teaching the children and young people the truths of Christianity is enough to fill the mind of the Christian with thankfulness and hope.

PULPIT AND PRESS.

It would be beyond the scope of an article of this character to attempt to recall the names of the eminent preachers of the century. It has been singularly rich in men of eloquence, depth of thought and high culture. A few, however, are distinguished among the noble army by the phenomenal character of their work. Of these probably no name is so widely known as that of Rev. T. DeWitt Talmage, D. D. One of the most remarkable phenomena of the religious world in this century, is the fact that every week one preacher should address an audience numbered by millions. The fact is unprecedented. Of all classes of readers, the number of those who read sermons is considered the smallest, yet this century has produced a preacher whose sermons command a public larger than that of a fascinating novelist. For thirty years the newspapers have been publishing Dr. Talmage's sermons in every city of his own land, in every English-speaking land and in many foreign lands where they are translated for publication. It is a significant fact, which should gratify every Christian, that the man whose words reach regularly and surely the largest audience in the world should be a preacher of the Gospel.

To no man in any walk of life, whether politician, editor or author, has the opportunity of impressing his thoughts on his generation that Dr. Talmage enjoys been given in such fulness. Next in extent of influence, and with a like faculty of reaching immense and widely scattered masses of people, was the late Charles Haddon Spurgeon, a preacher of singularly homely power, Calvinistic in theology, epigrammatic in style, and with an earnest evangelical spirit which had a powerful influence on both hearers and readers. His sermons, like those of Dr. Talmage, were read in every land and were instrumental in conversions wherever they went. Strongly resembling Mr. Spurgeon in his strong evangelicalism, as well as in homely eloquence, is Mr. D. L. Moody. During this century probably no man has addressed so large a number of people. In this country and in England such audiences have thronged the buildings in which he preached as no other orator has ever addressed on religious subjects, and the influence of his words is demonstrated by the thousands who through his appeals have been led to Christ.

We are nearing the end of the century. Looking back over the events in the religious world which have marked its history, one characteristic is prominent above all others. It is the operation of the force to which an eminent writer has given the name of "spiritual dynamics." The world does not need a dogma, or a creed, so much as it needs power. It needs power to live right, to do right, to love God and man, to pity the fallen, to relieve the needy, the power of being good, of leading a spiritual life. This power it finds in Christ, and the whole tendency of the religious life of the century is to get back to Him. Conduct rather than creed, love rather than theology, have been the watchwords of the Church. The spirit of Christ, His teachings, His character, His example, are the centre of attraction which holds His Church together and endues it with the power which shall yet subdue the world.

www.ingramcontent.com/pod-product-compliance
Lightning Source LLC
Chambersburg PA
CBHW011751220426
43671CB00017B/2944